Contents

Google Guice: Agile Lightweight Dependency Injection Framework

by Robbie Vanbrabant

Foreword by Bob Lee, Guice Lead

I created Guice in the midst of one of the biggest projects of my career. When you have hundreds of engineers touching millions of lines of code, you come to appreciate the benefits of static type checking. Static types aren't just about compiler errors. In fact, I rarely see Java compiler errors nowadays. Thanks to all that great, formalized Java type information, my IDE helps me write correct code in the first place.

Writing your application in a nearly 100 percent type safe manner, like Guice enables and Robbie advocates in this book, opens the door to a new level of maintainability. You can effortlessly navigate unfamiliar code, jumping from interfaces to their implementation and from methods to their callers. As you master your Java tools, you realize that deceptively simple atomic refactorings combine to form molecular tools, which you can reliably apply to companywide swaths of code, accomplishing refactorings you'd never even consider trying by hand. In the long run, it's much cheaper to ward off bit rot through heavy reuse and constant refactoring than by nuking the world with a rewrite every couple years.

Having experienced Guice's benefits on a number of projects, we at Google knew we couldn't keep it to ourselves and decided to make it open source. Readying Guice for the outside world felt like it took an order of magnitude more work than writing that first internal version, but community contributors like Robbie who fuel the forums, help polish rough edges, and generate excellent documentation like this book pay back that effort tenfold. You'll find that Robbie's brevity and conversational tone suit Guice well. I like my books like I like my APIs: with high power-to-weight ratios.

Chapter 1: Setting the Stage

You've probably heard about dependency injection (DI), and if so, you're in for a real treat: Guice (pronounced "juice") is, in my opinion, by far the most innovative framework in the problem space. Created by Google employees "Crazy" Bob Lee (http://crazybob.org) and Kevin Bourrillion (http://smallwig.blogspot.com), this lightweight, open source DI framework is designed to bring true ease of development to the world of DI. Taking advantage of Java 5 features like no other application has before, Guice is the XML-free cure to hard-to-maintain code.

Before I start talking about using frameworks, DI, and whatnot, I think it's best to step back and take a look why initiatives like Guice exist in the first place. Obviously, Guice is not the only DI framework out there. As with model-view-controller (MVC) web frameworks, there are lots of frameworks to choose from in the DI world, and everyone probably has their personal favorite. Whether or not you use Guice after reading this book will depend on your needs, but once you have a good grasp of the concepts described here, your code will never look the same again—whether you use Spring, PicoContainer, Guice, or no framework at all.

If this is the first time you've heard about DI, *don't worry*; this first chapter will explain, from the ground up, the problem at hand, and how Guice helps unravel the mystery of maintainable code. And who knows? This chapter might be a good refresher for experienced DI users.

The Problem

If you're in the business of creating software, you ultimately want to have maintainable software. You'll certainly agree with me that you spend more time maintaining software than writing software—and that the maintainability you need doesn't come for free. It requires careful design and a well defined process for testing and validating the application.

In your professional life, or even as a hobbyist, you've probably picked up the concept of unit testing. Basically, it's about testing little units of source code for validity. Being able to tell with one look at a bar (green or red) whether your code has the right side effects is valuable and will save you time. Unit testing is a no-brainer. In this book, unit test examples will use JUnit 4 (`http://www.junit.org`).

I strongly believe that automated testing, like unit testing, is the best way to achieve software maintainability. With the right amount of test coverage, you can rest assured that, when you're making changes to the code, you won't break code somewhere else in the code base. You can simply write your tests, make your change, run the collected set of tests, and feel confident. Poorly designed applications are usually hard to test, which means well tested applications probably aren't too bad. You *can* write great software without automated testing—you can also win the lottery, but don't count on it.

So there you have it: unit testing helps achieve maintainability. And what else can help you achieve that? Writing less code, of course! The less code you need to accomplish what you're trying to do, the less code you'll need to maintain. Obviously, you can't just randomly delete blocks of code, but in some cases, code doesn't really *mean* anything; it's just boilerplate to get you from point A to point B. Wouldn't it be nice if you could get rid of all that noise and focus on the stuff that matters? For lack of a better term, I call this the *maintainability mission statement*. This is not a complete list, but, among other things, maintainable code needs to be

- Easy to test (modular)
- Meaningful (as little noise as possible)

You probably already see where I'm going, but before we dive into Guice, let me illustrate how to accomplish these goals in a typical situation. When we're done with that, we'll throw Guice into the mix and dance on the ceiling.

A Fortunate Example

Let's say that the local Chinese restaurant has a new chef who insists on giving out fortune cookies with all the meals—you know, the ones that hold great advice or predictions. Now, the chef doesn't want to waste time in writing all these fortunes that could be spent preparing some delicious meals. That's where the fortune service comes in—the restaurant subscribes to a service that gives access to a rich database of fortunes. Listing 1-1 shows this fortune service's implementation.

Listing 1-1. FortuneService that Gives Out Fortunes

```
public interface FortuneService {
    String randomFortune();
}

public class FortuneServiceImpl implements FortuneService {
    private static final List<String> MESSAGES =
        Arrays.asList(
            "Today you will have some refreshing juice.",
            "Larry just bought your company."
        );

    public String randomFortune() {
        return MESSAGES.get(new Random().nextInt(MESSAGES.size()));
    }
}
```

For the chef, we're going to use the classic Gang of Four (GoF)[1] Factory pattern to create and retrieve the FortuneServiceImpl service. That way, we can easily swap in another FortuneService if we want. Listing 1-2 demonstrates this approach.

---

[1] *Design Patterns: Elements of Reusable Object-Oriented Software* by Erich Gamma, Richard Helm, Ralph Johnson, and John Vlissides (Addison-Wesley Professional, 1995) is widely known as the Gang of Four (GoF) book.

Listing 1-2. The Chef Uses a Factory (Hooray!)

```java
public class Chef {
    private FortuneService fortuneService;

    public Chef() {
        this.fortuneService = FortuneServiceFactory.getFortuneService();
    }

    public void makeFortuneCookie() {
        new FortuneCookie(fortuneService.randomFortune());
    }
}

public class FortuneServiceFactory {
    private FortuneServiceFactory() {}

    private static FortuneService fortuneService = new FortuneServiceImpl();

    public static FortuneService getFortuneService() {
        return fortuneService;
    }

    public static void setFortuneService(FortuneService mockFortuneService) {
        fortuneService = mockFortuneService;
    }
}
```

We can use the setter on the factory to swap in another implementation whenever we want. For example, we can change it to a mock implementation when testing the Chef class (see Listing 1-3). Note that as a side effect of this factory's implementation, the entire application now reuses the same FortuneService instance as long as nobody sets a different value for the service. It's a poor man's singleton (GoF Singleton pattern), if you will.

Tip: To learn more about mock objects, check out Martin Fowler's article at http://martinfowler.com/articles/mocksArentStubs.html.

Listing 1-3. Unit Test for the Chef Class

```java
public class ChefTest {
    @Test
    public void makeFortuneCookie() {
        final FortuneService original =
            FortuneServiceFactory.getFortuneService();
        try {
            FortuneServiceMock mock = new FortuneServiceMock();
            FortuneServiceFactory.setFortuneService(mock);
            Chef chef = new Chef();
            chef.makeFortuneCookie();
            assertTrue(mock.calledOnce());
        } finally {
            FortuneServiceFactory.setFortuneService(original);
        }

    }

    class FortuneServiceMock implements FortuneService {
        private int invocationCount;

        public String randomFortune() {
            invocationCount++;
            return "MOCK";
        }

        public boolean calledOnce() {
            return invocationCount == 1;
        }
    }
}
```

Although this works, you've probably seen better looking code. We have to be
careful to clean up the factory when we're done using the `finally` block. If we
don't, other tests in the same suite might receive the value we put in for our test
and fail, because they depend on a different value. Let's see how DI tackles this
kind of problem.

Dependency Injection

In the last five years, there's been a lot of buzz around inversion of control (IoC)
and DI. Looking past all the silly terminology, using DI frequently means that,
instead of pulling your dependencies in, you opt to *receive* them from someplace,

and you don't care where they come from. People often explain it as the Hollywood principle—don't call us; we'll call you. So, for the example given, the Chef class could receive the FortuneService as a constructor parameter. This has several advantages:

- Your dependencies are immediately visible by looking at the class structure.

- It's easy to use multiple FortuneService implementations *within the same application* now.

- You get rid of a static method invocation on a factory, which is always a good thing. Static method calls are hard to test, because you can't change the actual behavior as you can with interfaces. It didn't matter all that much for this example, but it always feels good to eliminate a static method.

- Test cases are simpler to write, as you'll see in this section.

Note: As you'll see, you don't need to have a framework to make use of the DI idiom. For more information on these concepts, again, Martin Fowler has a great article on his web site describing the ins and outs: http://martinfowler.com/articles/injection.html. Buy the man's books; they're all classics. It might also be worth noting that all the things we are discussing (factories and DI) are basically workarounds to problems in the Java programming language itself. Gilad Bracha, former Sun employee and coauthor of the Java Language Specification, explains why in his blog posts "Constructors Considered Harmful" (http://gbracha.blogspot.com/2007/06/constructors-considered-harmful.html) and "Lethal Injection" (http://gbracha.blogspot.com/2007/12/some-months-ago-i-wrote-couple-of-posts.html).

Listing 1-4 contains the Chef class, modified to use DI.

Listing 1-4. Chef Goes DI

```
public class Chef {
    private final FortuneService fortuneService;

    public Chef(FortuneService fortuneService) {
```

```
        this.fortuneService = fortuneService;
    }

    public void makeFortuneCookie() {
        new FortuneCookie(fortuneService.randomFortune());
    }
}
```

Because I am now able to get rid of the factory, the unit test code also looks a lot simpler (see Listing 1-5). Josh Bloch, *Effective Java* author (Prentice Hall, 2001), would probably say: "Code should read like prose." High five, Josh; we're on our way!

Listing 1-5. Unit Testing Chef, DI style

```
public class ChefTest {
    @Test
    public void makeFortuneCookie() {
        FortuneServiceMock mock = new FortuneServiceMock();
        Chef chef = new Chef(mock);
        chef.makeFortuneCookie();
        assertTrue(mock.calledOnce());
    }
}
```

One thing that doesn't immediately surface with a small example like this is that we didn't *solve* the factory problem. Although our test case now looks much simpler, eventually you're going to have to write a factory for the Chef class to provide its FortuneService dependency, so we've only moved the factory problem higher up the stack (see Listing 1-6).

Listing 1-6. The Revenge of the Chef

```
public class ChefFactory {
    public Chef newChef() {
        return new Chef(FortuneServiceFactory.getFortuneService());
    }
}
```

Now, how can we get rid of *those* factories, Batman? On to the latest and greatest option—drum roll—Google Guice!

DI, Guice Style

With Guice, instead of writing factories to wire up things, you write a small amount of configuration that's reusable across the entire application. By handing off all object wiring responsibilities to Guice, you'll effectively have DI without the factories.

First, you put the Guice @Inject annotation at the injection point, as shown in Listing 1-7. It's like saying, "Here's where I want your help!"

Listing 1-7. Guicy Chef

```java
public class Chef {
    private final FortuneService fortuneService;

    @Inject
    public Chef(FortuneService fortuneService) {
        this.fortuneService = fortuneService;
    }

    public void makeFortuneCookie() {
        new FortuneCookie(fortuneService.randomFortune());
    }
}
```

Our unit test, shown in Listing 1-8, stays exactly the same:

Listing 1-8. Unit Testing Chef, Guice Style (No Changes!)

```java
public class ChefTest {
    @Test
    public void makeFortuneCookie() {
        FortuneServiceMock mock = new FortuneServiceMock();
        Chef chef = new Chef(mock);
        chef.makeFortuneCookie();
        assertTrue(mock.calledOnce());
    }
}
```

The only thing left is to tell Guice which implementation to use for FortuneService. You do this by defining a *module*. I'll go into the details in the next chapter, but for now, Listing 1-9 shows you one possible approach.

Listing 1-9. Guice Module for the Chef Class's Dependency

```java
public class ChefModule implements Module {
```

```
public void configure(Binder binder) {
    binder.bind(FortuneService.class)
            .to(FortuneServiceImpl.class)
            .in(Scopes.SINGLETON);
}
}
```

Easy, huh? You implement a single-method interface and get a `Binder` object to play with. This `Binder` uses a special syntax designed to make your configuration easy to read. If you read from left to right, you get "bind `FortuneService` to `FortuneServiceImpl` in singleton scope." Guice will figure out how to do the rest.

Compared to manual DI, using a framework like Guice has several advantages:

- You can take advantage of automated object lifetimes (singleton scope, in this example). Remember the manual singleton when using the factory? (See Listing 1-2.)

- Because you don't express object-wiring code directly in your code, you can easily reuse or replace it across the application and beyond.

- You're able to catch missing or wrong dependency mistakes early.

- Once objects are in the club, meaning the framework controls their creation and lifetime, you can do all sorts of things with them, like apply aspect-oriented programming (AOP) advice (http://www.ibm.com/developerworks/ java/library/j-aspectj/). Guice's lightweight AOP will be introduced in Chapter 4, "Aspect-Oriented Programming."

- You write less code.

- A carefully crafted framework will help you fall into the "pit of success."

Let me quote Rico Mariani, Microsoft performance guru, to explain this last statement.

> *In stark contrast to a summit, peak, or a journey across a desert to find victory through many trials and surprises, we want our customers to simply fall into winning practices by using our platform and frameworks. To the extent that we make it easy to get into trouble we fail.*

> —*Framework Design Guidelines* (Addison-Wesley Professional, 2005)

Much like in Rico Mariani's statement, the Guice authors went out of their way to make sure that they designed the framework in such a way that it's easy to do the right thing and much harder to shoot yourself in the foot. They killed a whole class of bugs for you.

Tip: Use tools like FindBugs to hunt down the remaining bugs (`http://findbugs.sf.net`).

Last but not least, unlike other DI frameworks, Guice gives you all of those listed advantaged while you're using *pure, elegant Java*. To see how that looks, let's move on to Chapter 2.

Summary

We live in an age where writing software to a given set of requirements is no longer enough. We need to write *maintainable* software that is easy to test and easy to read. These days, we spend a lot more time reading, changing, and reusing existing code than writing new code.

Testable code allows us to swap in different implementations of expensive services or dependencies currently not under test. Traditionally, we've been using the GoF Factory pattern to abstract object creation, but having to write all that factory code is tedious. On the other hand, using dependency injection (DI) makes your code easier to test but still doesn't let you get rid of all the boilerplate factory code. This is where frameworks like Guice come in: using an applicationwide configuration, you describe how your DI-style code is wired together.

The rest of this book will explain the core Guice concepts using small and not-so-small examples.

Chapter 2: Enter Guice

Now that I've told you why this book exists, let's talk about the actual Guice technology. The goal of this chapter is to give you a basic understanding of what you need to do to use Guice in your projects. You'll want to set up your development environment so that you can try these examples as we go through them, so I'll briefly cover that in the first section. Once you're past that, I'll help you think your way through your first Guice adventure.

Getting Guice

Like most open source software, Guice is freely downloadable on the Internet. However, before you download Guice, make sure that you have the following installed:

- Java Development Kit (JDK) for Java 5 or above
  (http://www.java.com/getjava)

- Eclipse (http://www.eclipse.org) or your Java IDE of choice

Once you have that, you're finally ready to slurp up some Guice.

1. Go to http://code.google.com/p/google-guice.
2. Click the Downloads tab.
3. Download the file named guice-1.0.zip.
4. Unzip the archive to a directory of your choice.

Inside the archive, you'll find the Guice API documentation and, as shown in Table 2-1, several JAR files. Now, we only need guice-1.0.jar, which holds the core framework. The other ones are either dependencies or extensions.

Table 2-1. Guice 1.0 Download Contents

FILE	DESCRIPTION
guice-1.0.jar	The core Guice framework
guice-spring-1.0.jar	Spring Framework integration functionality (bind Spring beans)
guice-servlet-1.0.jar	Web-related scope additions
guice-struts2-plugin-1.0.jar	Plug-in to use Guice as the DI engine for Struts 2
aopalliance.jar	AOP Alliance API, needed to use Guice AOP

To follow along with the code examples in this chapter, create a new Java project in your IDE, and add guice-1.0.jar to the class path. Note that because some code listings only show the code relevant to the given section, some examples will not run as they are, but trying out the examples will definitely give you a good feel for how Guice works.

Preparing the Code

Let's revisit the example we used in the first chapter. Remember how I tagged the Chef constructor with @Inject? Take a look at Listing 2-1 for a refresher.

Listing 2-1. Chef, Tagged with @Inject

```
public class Chef {
    private final FortuneService fortuneService;

    @Inject
    public Chef(FortuneService fortuneService) {
        this.fortuneService = fortuneService;
    }

    public void makeFortuneCookie() {
        new FortuneCookie(fortuneService.randomFortune());
    }
}
```

Tagging a constructor with @Inject is essentially telling Guice where you want a dependency to be provided for you. Not only does this work for constructors but you can also apply @Inject to fields or methods.

Which style you choose depends on the class's requirements and arguably your personal taste. Table 2-2 sums up your choices.

Table 2-2. Guice Injection Styles

Location	Injection Order	Motivation	Comment
Constructor	First	Class immutability[1] Mandatory dependencies	Only one allowed with @Inject.
Field	Second	Quick prototyping Code that doesn't need testing	Injection order is random.
Setter	Third	Dealing with legacy classes Optional dependencies[2]	Injection order is random.

1. Remember that immutability also means thread safety.

2. The @Inject annotation has an optional property, which is set to false by default but can be set to true, which tells Guice to ignore values for which there are no bindings available. This applies to the entire injection point though. so or you make all setter parameters optional, or you can isolate optional dependencies using a different setter method for each parameter. Depending on the situation, you could also favor injecting an empty dummy object, also known as using the Null Object design pattern. In that case there is no need to set the optional property to true. That said, this optional property also works when using field injection, but obviously not when injecting constructors.

By "injection order is random," I mean that you should not rely on the order of injection. For example, if your class had two setters tagged with @Inject, you will never be sure which one will get called first by Guice. Guice often *appears* to use the order in which the methods were declared, but injection order can vary depending on the JVM you use, so assume the order is random.

Setter injection is a concept that is often misunderstood. If you're used accustomed to using Spring, you've been probably using what *it* calls setter injection—effectively, injection of JavaBean-style setters, which mean the methods you want to inject should be named setXXX, where XXX is the name of the single property that needs mutating. Guice, however, does not depend on this naming convention and can handle multiple parameters. The reasoning behind this is that it's also valid to want to inject methods that don't mutate a property but, for example, execute some kind of initialization logic right after object creation. But know that, as with Spring's setter injection, methods marked for injection get called with the appropriate values right after Guice creates the object for you. Once the object is fully initialized, Guice gets out of the way, and no more magic happens. So when you call the method yourself later, Guice does *not* magically provide some value for you.

What does work when it comes to injection is inheritance. If you subclass a class that features @Inject annotations, injection works as expected. First, the superclass gets injected, then the subclass. This only works for concrete classes though; you can't tag an implemented interface's members with @Inject and cross your fingers. Well you can, but it's not going to work.

It's also possible to inject static members or even members on objects that Guice didn't construct, but there's more on that in the next chapter.

One final interesting point to note is that whichever type of injection you use, the target's visibility does not matter. Guice will inject anything tagged with @Inject whether it's private, package private, protected, or public.

Caution: Guice's ability to inject regardless of visibility can come in handy, but remember that injecting into private members is usually not needed and probably a bad idea. Unless you're injecting a public member, always think twice, "Is there a public member by which I can achieve the same?" Or in the case of private members, "Is it fine to cripple this class's testability?" Field injection especially is a frequent offender, because fields are typically private. If your class is important enough to need testing, it should be possible to change its state without resorting to nasty reflection tricks for bypassing its visibility. Don't depend on Guice being there; in fact, unit tests shouldn't need Guice at all.

Next up, I need to tell Guice that the chef wants a FortuneServiceImpl object when a FortuneService is requested.

Specifying an Implementation

Using the Module subclass I made previously, I can tell Guice which implementation to use for the Chef class's FortuneService, as illustrated in Listing 2-2.

Listing 2-2. Telling Guice Which FortuneService Service to Use

```
public class ChefModule implements Module {
    public void configure(Binder binder) {
        binder.bind(FortuneService.class)
            .to(FortuneServiceImpl.class);
    }
}
```

You can also subclass the AbstractModule abstract class instead of implementing Module. This abstract class implements Module itself and exposes a no-argument configure() method. To purists, using AbstractModule probably looks a bit scarier than implementing the actual interface, but it's more concise.

Listing 2-3. AbstractModule Saves You Some Keystrokes

```
public class ChefModule extends AbstractModule {
    protected void configure() {
        bind(FortuneService.class).to(FortuneServiceImpl.class);
    }
}
```

I'll explain more about the binder syntax and modules in Chapter 3, "From Journeyman to Bob."

Bootstrapping

To start using Guice, you create an instance of Injector . This central Guice type takes a collected set of Module implementations and injects our beloved Chef class. To create the Injector, I use one of the factory methods on the Guice class, which is a simple static class, to serve as a starting point for creating injectors. This method, createInjector(...), takes a varargs argument, which means you can specify zero or more modules, separated by a comma. For Chef, I only need one. I'll have one cookie, please. Listing 2-4 to the rescue!

Listing 2-4. Bootstrapping Guice and Creating Chef

```
public class FortuneApplication {
    public static void main(String[] args) {
        Injector i = Guice.createInjector(new ChefModule());
        Chef chef = i.getInstance(Chef.class);
        chef.makeFortuneCookie();
    }
}
```

FortuneServiceImpl doesn't have any dependencies itself, but if it did, Guice would have resolved its dependencies too. This recursive behavior allows you to use the Injector somewhere high up the stack in your application; Guice will then create the entire graph of dependencies below a requested object recursively.

The core Guice team has been reluctant to call this class a container, as you would probably expect it to be named. Naming it Container would make you think that your objects sit somewhere in a container being managed, having a life cycle, and what not, which is not the way Guice does DI. The Injector injects your objects, and from then on, you're in control.

Note: You will want to minimize the dependency on the Injector to avoid having a direct dependency on Guice. This is usually not very hard to do, as I'll show in Chapter 5.

If you look around a bit, you'll see that createInjector(...) also has an overload that takes a Stage enumeration as the first parameter. The Stage of the Injector defines the mode of operation.

Using Stage.DEVELOPMENT means you'll have a faster start-up time and better error reporting at the cost of run-time performance and some up-front error checking. Stage.DEVELOPMENT is also the default. Using Stage.PRODUCTION on the other hand (shown in Listing 2-5), catches errors as early as possible and takes the full performance hit at start-up. But don't worry; Guice's overall performance is surprisingly good anyway. Just don't forget to switch on `Stage.PRODUCTION` for production code.

Listing 2-5. Specifying a Stage for the Injector

```
Injector i = Guice.createInjector(Stage.PRODUCTION, new ChefModule());
```

Choosing Between Implementations

The chef was obviously not pleased to figure out that the `FortuneServiceImpl` only had two fortunes to offer. To get some more variation in the messages, our chef subscribes to a second service, the `MegaFortuneService`, shown in Listing 2-6. Because the original subscription doesn't end until the end of the year, some way to choose between the two is necessary.

Listing 2-6. MegaFortuneService

```
public class MegaFortuneService implements FortuneService {
    private static final List<FortuneService> SERVICES =
        Arrays.<FortuneService>asList(
            new FunnyFortuneService(),
            new QuoteFortuneService()
        );

    public String randomFortune() {
        int index = new Random().nextInt(SERVICES.size());
        return SERVICES.get(index).randomFortune();
    }
}
```

Previously, the Guice knew which `FortuneService` to inject for `Chef`, because we had a binding in a `Module` implementation (see Listing 2-2). Common sense tells me to just add another binding for `MegaFortuneService`. Listing 2-7 shows what I came up with.

Listing 2-7. Adding Another Binding: Does This Work?

```
public class CommonSenseModule extends AbstractModule {
    protected void configure() {
        bind(FortuneService.class).to(FortuneServiceImpl.class);
        bind(FortuneService.class).to(MegaFortuneService.class);
    }
}
```

You can easily modify the code in Listing 2-4 to create the `Injector` with the `Module` from Listing 2-7. However, when you do, you'll notice that Guice blows up at start-up. You'd see something like Listing 2-8.

Listing 2-8. Oops, I Did It Again

```
Exception in thread "main" com.google.inject.CreationException:
Guice configuration errors:
1) Error at chapter2.CommonSenseModule.configure(CommonSenseModule.java:12):
A binding to chapter1.FortuneService was already configured at
 chapter2.CommonSenseModule.configure(CommonSenseModule.java:11).
```

Oh man, Guice doesn't like that. What did I forget? If you take a second look at the `Chef` constructor, shown in Listing 2-9, you'll see.

Note: Guice's exceptions comprise a feature on their own. They go the extra mile and present you a human readable message and line numbers from your configuration code where appropriate. You'll be pleasantly surprised.

Listing 2-9. The Chef Constructor

```
@Inject
public Chef(FortuneService fortuneService) {
    this.fortuneService = fortuneService;
}
```

Of course! Guice can't tell which `FortuneService` we need for `Chef`! So even if Guice would allow our `CommonSenseModule` bindings, using them would have never worked, because Guice has two `FortuneService` instances to choose from. I need some way to tell Guice, "Give me the `MegaFortuneService`!" without having to use the concrete implementations directly.

Instead of letting you write more configuration, Guice solves this problem elegantly using binding annotations. Listing 2-10 provides an example.

Listing 2-10. The Chef Constructor with a Binding Annotation

```
@Inject
public Chef(@Mega FortuneService fortuneService) {
    this.fortuneService = fortuneService;
}
```

Now I can tell Guice which service is which in a module, as shown in Listing 2-11.

Listing 2-11. A Module Using Binding Annotations

```
public class BindingAnnotationModule extends AbstractModule {
    protected void configure() {
        bind(FortuneService.class).to(FortuneServiceImpl.class);
        bind(FortuneService.class)
            .annotatedWith(Mega.class)
            .to(MegaFortuneService.class);
    }
}
```

Again, my configuration remains highly readable, "Bind all requests for FortuneService annotated with @Mega to MegaFortuneService."

One might hope that Guice provides these binding annotations for you. Alas, that wouldn't work for the same reason actors shouldn't go into politics: sometimes, you just have absolutely no idea what you're talking about. Similarly, Guice can't possibly know how to name your binding annotations, what their visibility should be, or where you would want to place them (in a constructor, method, or so on). That's why you need to create them yourself, much like in the @Mega example in Listing 2-12. Most binding annotations look very similar, so don't feel bad copying and pasting the boilerplate code. In fact, I even recommend doing so, because that means you're less likely to forget something.

Listing 2-12. @Mega Binding Annotation

```
@Retention(RetentionPolicy.RUNTIME)
@Target({ElementType.FIELD, ElementType.PARAMETER})
@BindingAnnotation
public @interface Mega {}
```

Scary stuff. Table 2-3 explains what all that gibberish means.

Table 2-3. Binding Annotation, Line by Line

CODE	EXPLANATION
`@Retention(RetentionPolicy.RUNTIME)`	The annotation should be discoverable at run time.
`@Target({ElementType.Field, ElementType.PARAMETER})`	This is where the annotation can appear.
`@BindingAnnotation`	This tells Guice that this is a binding annotation.
`public @interface Mega {}`	The actual annotation is declared.

To support this binding annotation functionality, Guice internally identifies all bindings with an instance of the Key class. A Key instance is a combination of a type (FortuneService) and an optional annotation type (@Mega). If you played around with the Injector a bit in the previous section, you probably noticed that the getInstance(...) method has an overload that takes a Key object instead of a Class one. There's only one Chef, but if you would like to get a MegaFortuneService directly, you would do so as in Listing 2-13.

Listing 2-13. Getting an Instance by its Key

```
injector.getInstance(Key.get(FortuneService.class, Mega.class));
```

If you call getInstance(...) with a Class, for example, Chef.class, Guice actually delegates to getInstance(Key) internally. So the two lines in Listing 2-14 are essentially the same.

Listing 2-14. Get by Class or by Key

```
injector.getInstance(Chef.class);
injector.getInstance(Key.get(Chef.class));
```

Understanding that every single binding is internally represented by a Key object, including simple class bindings like Chef, will save you lots of time. Especially when you start using Guice's object lifetime support (scopes). I can't emphasize this enough, so repeat it after me: *Every binding is represented by a* Key, *the whole* Key *and nothing but the* Key, *so help me Bob.*

Implicit Bindings

In the fortunes example, you've probably noticed that I never made an explicit binding for Chef. This is because bindings don't always have to be explicit. As a rule of thumb, if there is no ambiguity, Guice will figure it out for you. This applies to concrete classes. As shown in Listing 2-15, I could have configured an explicit binding to Chef. This is kind of redundant, so I usually don't bind concrete classes explicitly.

Listing 2-15. Explicit Binding for Chef

```
public class ExplicitChefModule extends AbstractModule {
    protected void configure() {
        // no to(…) because you can't bind to the same class
        bind(Chef.class);
    }
}
```

Next to these implicit bindings, provided by Guice, you can also reduce configuration yourself when working with interfaces. Guice comes with an @ImplementedBy annotation that lets you specify which concrete class implementation to use for an interface. For example, Listing 2-16 shows the same FortuneService interface from Listing 2-2, now changed to use @ImplementedBy.

Listing 2-16. Using @ImplementedBy

```
@ImplementedBy(FortuneServiceImpl.class)
public interface FortuneService {
    String randomFortune();
}
```

By using @ImplementedBy, you can get rid of modules altogether. Whether that's a good idea or not, I'll leave up to you to decide. I usually stick to modules, because they allow you to change your application's configuration in a single line of code, by including or excluding certain modules when creating the Injector. However, you can use @ImplementedBy to specify a default implementation, and then override it in a Module implementation. That way, when creating an Injector without any modules, you'll always get a default implementation.

Note: `Module` configuration *always* takes precedence over annotation configuration.

Scoping

Guice's default behavior is to create a new instance of an object each time that object gets requested or injected. Scopes allow you to customize an object's lifetime. The canonical example is the built-in singleton scope, which makes sure only one instance of an object exists for a given `Injector` and internal `Key`. This is much, much better than using singletons manually, because this does not involve using static factory methods (or writing any code at all). But, as with any singleton, you'll have to make sure that your class is thread safe if you're going to access it from multiple threads.

To apply a scope to our `FortuneService` bindings, we specify either a scope annotation or an instance of the `Scope` class. For a singleton, these are `Singleton.class` and `Scopes.SINGLETON` respectively. In Listing 2-17, I mix both of these styles (not recommended).

Listing 2-17. Using Two Styles to Apply a Scope

```
public class ScopedModule extends AbstractModule {
    protected void configure() {
        bind(FortuneService.class)
            .to(FortuneServiceImpl.class)
            .in(Singleton.class);
        bind(FortuneService.class)
            .annotatedWith(Mega.class)
            .to(MegaFortuneService.class)
            .in(Scopes.SINGLETON);
    }
}
```

In the next chapter, I'll show you that it's almost always better to bind to the annotation instead of binding to the `Scope` instance directly.

You can also apply a scope by directly tagging your class with the `@Singleton` annotation, but as with `@ImplementedBy`, bindings in modules always take precedence.

The question that now is, "Do singletons load lazily or eagerly?" The short answer is that this will depend on the Injector's Stage, as I mentioned earlier. If you want to make sure that your singleton is created at application start-up (loaded eagerly), regardless of the Injector's Stage or the binding's usage, you can specify that as in Listing 2-18.

Tip: Stage.PRODUCTION loads singletons eagerly; Stage.DEVELOPMENT does not.

Listing 2-18. Eager Singleton Loading

```
public class EagerSingletonModule extends AbstractModule {
    protected void configure() {
        bind(FortuneService.class)
            .to(FortuneServiceImpl.class)
            .asEagerSingleton();
        bind(FortuneService.class)
            .annotatedWith(Mega.class)
            .to(MegaFortuneService.class)
            .asEagerSingleton();
    }
}
```

Loading singletons eagerly might be useful to execute initialization logic for your application. You can even create dependencies between them in such a way that you're sure they'll come up in the right order.

I've only talked about the singleton scope for now, because it's the only scope that ships with core Guice (guice-1.0.jar). The 1.0 distribution also comes with a guice-servlet-1.0.jar archive containing the web-specific (servlet-specific) scopes: request and session. I'll talk about those in the next chapter; I promise.

Debunking Myths

Before finishing up in this chapter, let's investigate a couple of common myths that haunt Guice. Some people who've seen the core Guice concepts, like you have now, are not entirely comfortable with them. It seems like a pretty good framework, but it still seems to leave a weird taste in the mouth. In my experience, the reason is often twofold. Take a look at the following statements:

- Annotations seem to be intrusive and introduce tight coupling.

- The Spring Framework has done what Guice does for years.

The first statement is simply not true. There's an interesting discussion on this on Bob Lee's blog (`http://crazybob.org/2007/06/lies-damned-lies-and-xml.html`) that describes why. I'll summarize it for you here. Let's start off with Kevin Bourrillion's words on annotations from `http://smallwig.blogspot.com/2007/06/coupling.html`: "They do absolutely nothing to impede you from testing your code, or from using the classes with Spring."

Bob Lee goes on to add that you can easily create a separate Guice integration package for your application if you don't want a compile-time dependency on Guice. Though SpringSource's Colin Sampaleanu argued that you'd still need the Guice JAR on your classpath when migrating to another framework because you're using Guice annotations in your code, in reality, this is a nonissue. Here's why:

- Annotations don't do anything; they're just metadata. Is JavaDoc intrusive if you mention Guice in it? As Kevin also points out in the blog post I quoted above, tight coupling would mean that "one cannot function without the other". Annotations do not introduce this kind of coupling.

- Technically speaking, you can get rid of the annotations in your application's compiled `.class` files. Just provide your own versions of the Guice annotations that don't have `Retention.RUNTIME` set.

Note: At this point, people often argue that Guice should make it possible for users to configure their own annotation, instead of @Inject. This appears to be a good idea, but it wouldn't buy you anything. Even if you were using your own annotations, you would still have them in your code, because you want to use Guice. I don't see how that's any different to using Guice's @Inject. On the other hand, that feature would enable Guice to make use of EJB 3's @Resource annotations, for example. That's a valid use case, but as you'll see in the last chapter, there will be a more general way to enable this kind flexibility in a future Guice release.

I think the conclusion is simple. Some people hate it when JavaDoc pollutes their code; others don't. The annotations debate is, in my opinion, a matter of taste and *nothing more*. There is no solid technical argument against the use of annotations.

Let's move on to the second statement, which asserts that the Spring Framework has done what Guice does for years. That's true, as long as you're talking about the DI idiom in general. But there are some differences that you should be aware of.

First, the Spring Framework still heavily depends on XML configuration. Your configuration, containing object wiring as well as other properties, is externalized by default when using the framework. In more recent versions of the framework, notably version 2.5, Spring *has* added support for annotation-driven object wiring. Unfortunately, you will probably still end up defining your beans in XML. You *can* get away with a single line of XML if you really want to, but that mode of operation requires you to put your bean configuration directly on the beans themselves, which is not as flexible as, say, using Guice modules. Alternatively, you can also use the JavaConfig option, but that feels like writing XML in Java. Anyway, my advice is to stay away from Spring's annotation-driven configuration options altogether. If you're going to use Spring, use the XML. It's the best documented option, and tools like Spring IDE are good enough to compensate for a lot of the annoyances.

With Guice your configuration will be done in Java by default, with externalized properties as an option (see Chapter 3). Externalized object wiring configuration is highly overrated and often not worth the added complexity and tooling dependencies. When was the last time you *really* changed your object wiring after deployment?

Note: I should mention that you can and probably should solve your Guice dynamic object wiring needs, if any, by loading modules dynamically and *not* by fully externalizing configuration in a custom file format or scripting language (like Ruby). Chapter 5 discusses this option in the "Configuration Discovery" section.

Second, because Guice uses Java as its primary configuration option, its modules also get some things for free:

- There's no need to use tooling other than a Java IDE.
- Java's type safety means that the compiler catches a lot of your mistakes early.
- You get Java's documentation standard, JavaDoc.
- You also get Java's test frameworks, like JUnit.

As Bob Lee likes to put it, types are the natural currency of Java since version 5 of the platform.

Third, Guice is much smaller, is easier to learn and use, and has a much better power to complexity ratio than Spring. For an example of Guice's simplicity, I urge you to take a look at Guice AOP (explained in Chapter 4). The Spring Framework, however, definitely has its value, including full-featured integration with lots of open source and commercial products and various Java Enterprise Edition (Java EE) standards. I've used Spring in the past and will probably continue to use it. Guice is not the new Spring and doesn't try to be. In fact, as I'll demonstrate in Chapter 7, there's no reason why both can't coexist.

Last but not least, let me emphasize that Guice is a DI framework, not a full-stack application framework like Spring. Comparing them in terms of feature set is like comparing apples and oranges. Use the frameworks that fit your needs.

Summary

I've given you lots to think about in this chapter. Now that you have most of the basic building blocks, you're ready to stop eating fortune cookies and dive into the advanced functionality. Let me recap what you've seen so far.

To use Guice, besides using a DI style of programming, you generally do the following:

- Tag your classes with @Inject and an optional binding annotation wherever you want Guice to provide a dependency for you.

- Tell Guice which implementation you want as a dependency. If it's not an implicit binding (a concrete class or through annotation configuration), specify those bindings in an implementation of Module.

- Make sure that your bindings are scoped correctly. Scopes define the binding's instances lifetimes.

- Create the Injector with the modules you've created, and get an instance of any class Guice knows about.

You also learned that

- Annotations are not evil.

- Both the Spring and Guice frameworks have their strengths.

And remember: every binding is represented by a Key, the whole Key and nothing but the Key, so help me Bob.

Chapter 3: From Journeyman to Bob

Now that you're familiar with the Guice basics, you're ready to go become a Guice master: scope like no one has scoped before; the world is at your Injector; the annotations lay at your feet, and so on—unless, of course, you skipped the previous chapter, you rascal.

Seriously, although you have a good understanding of what Guice is about, you still need that little bit of extra know-how to get going. Not everything you code against will implement an interface or will have a DI-style design, and you need to be prepared to deal with that. Also, Guice has some handy shortcuts when it comes to, for example, handling constant values or injecting configuration from a properties file. In this chapter, I'll stick all that in a giant blender with some best practices and, heaven forbid, some more theory and serve it to you, ice cold.

Providers

When you request an object from Guice, it looks for a suitable constructor and executes it. However, sometimes this simple construction mechanism doesn't cut it:

- You want to delay new object construction until some point in time in your code execution, instead of using a direct dependency. For example, client code gets to decide which database to use, and you don't want to connect to all of them right away.

- You need multiple instances of a class. For example, a GumballMachine class would give out multiple instances of the same Gum type.

- You want to give out your own managed instance of a class. Often the same result can be achieved using scopes (more on scopes later in this chapter), but there are cases where using a Provider feels more natural.

- You need an instance of a type that is expensive to create or has a fair chance of throwing an exception during creation. To isolate this risk, more control over object creation can be desirable.

- You're using a third-party API that you can't modify directly (can't add `@Inject`).

- You're working with legacy code that, for example, depends on a factory class or method for object construction.

To overcome these problems, Guice has the concept of a `Provider`. Instead of binding to an implementation, you bind to an implementation of the single method interface shown in Listing 3-1.

Listing 3-1. The Provider Interface

```
public interface Provider<T> {
    T get();
}
```

A `Provider` implementation is basically a small factory class that Guice will invoke whenever it needs an instance of the given type.

Let's configure a provider for the `GumballMachine` scenario described previously; see Listing 3-2.

Listing 3-2. Provider-Backed Gum

```
public class Gum {}

public class GumballMachine {
    @Inject
    private Provider<Gum> gumProvider;

    public Gum dispense() {
        return gumProvider.get();
    }
}

public class GumProvider implements Provider<Gum> {
    public Gum get() {
        return new Gum();
    }
}

public class GumModule extends AbstractModule {
    protected void configure() {
        bind(Gum.class).toProvider(GumProvider.class);
    }
}
```

```
public class GumballExample {
    public static void main(String[] args) {
        Injector injector = Guice.createInjector(new GumModule());
        GumballMachine m = injector.getInstance(GumballMachine.class);
        System.out.println(m.dispense());
        System.out.println(m.dispense());
    }
}
```

Running the GumballExample class will show you that it returns two distinct instances, for example:

```
Gum@10f11b8
Gum@544ec1
```

Because Guice implicitly makes a Provider instance available for all bindings (including implicit bindings), I could have dropped the use of the GumModule altogether (thus not using GumProvider):

```
public class GumballExample {
    public static void main(String[] args) {
        Injector injector = Guice.createInjector();
        GumballMachine m = injector.getInstance(GumballMachine.class);
        System.out.println(m.dispense());
        System.out.println(m.dispense());
    }
}
```

Now, what if Gum itself needs some dependency? Well, you can inject into providers like any other class. But you'll need to define one provider explicitly, like I did earlier. For example, you could apply a color to a Gum (if there's a binding for color, at least) as shown in Listing 3-3.

Listing 3-3. Injecting into a Provider

```
public class BlueGumProvider implements Provider<Gum> {
    @Inject Color color;
    public Gum get() {
        return new Gum(color);
    }
}
```

Notice that I'm using field injection in these examples. Usually, you shouldn't feel guilty about using field injection in providers; they don't need testing anyway. Reconsider, however, when the Provider will be hit by multiple threads concurrently. In such cases, using constructor injection combined with final fields is a much more robust option. The same goes for all your other objects, actually. If you want to learn about safe publication or concurrency in general, I highly recommend *Java Concurrency in Practice* by Brian Goetz, Tim Peierls, Joshua Bloch, Joseph Bowbeer, David Holmes, and Doug Lea (Addison-Wesley Professional, 2006). If your providers or other objects are not thread safe, make sure that's on purpose.

Tip: If you're ever dying to pass in a parameter to one of your Provider instances, you should probably consider rolling your own intermediate class (using the GoF's Builder pattern) or take a look at AssistedInject (http://publicobject.com/2007/06/assistedinject-easier-way-to-help-guice.html). The latter will probably make its way into Guice 2.0 in some form. Also, when working with lots of legacy classes, take a look this post on Tim Peierls's blog: http://tembrel.blogspot.com/2007/04/guice-utility-for-binding-to-legacy.html.

Before we move on to the next section, consider a final quick fact: much like @ImplementedBy, there's also an @ProvidedBy annotation that let's you slap a Provider directly on a type. Because both concepts are so similar, I'm not going to present an example here, but know the capability is there and that it's there for a similar purpose—defaulting.

For more examples on Provider usage, see Chapters 6 and 7.

@Named

Unlike rain, binding annotations don't coming falling out of the sky. But besides crafting your own custom binding annotations, there's also the option of reusing a single annotation called @Named. This annotation uses a string identifier to differentiate among different bindings. While using @Named comes at the cost of less type safety, it sometimes makes sense to avoid writing a bunch of annotations to get things going, which you'll find particularly useful when prototyping a piece of code or creating a large number of bindings automatically.

To use @Named, simply tag your injection point and specify a string identifier, as shown in Listing 3-4.

Listing 3-4. Using @Named

```
public class ActionMovie {
    @Inject @Named("stallone")
    private Actor actor;
}
```

There's something notable about how you would bind this—the code in Listing 3-5 appears to work but is not correct.

Listing 3-5. Binding @Named, the Wrong Way

```
bind(Actor.class).annotatedWith(Named.class).to(...);
```

Besides matching the Actor for our ActionMovie, the line in Listing 3-5 would match *every* Actor *in the universe* who has been tagged with @Named! Imagine all the actors looking like Sly. Seriously, you need some way to specify the name of the actor in the binding. To do that, you bind to an annotation generated by Guice's named(...) utility method on the Names class.

Listing 3-6. Binding @Named, the Right Way

```
bind(Actor.class).annotatedWith(Names.named("stallone")).to(...);
```

Note: The named(...) method generates a subclass of the @Named annotation on which Guice can match internally, because you can't create an instance of an annotation directly—clever stuff to think about.

There you have it. Remember to use @Named sparingly; there's nothing protecting you from typos in string identifiers, but it is *da bomb* for examples or quick prototyping code.

Binding Constants

Guice also features a shorthand syntax for binding constant values, which is presented in Listing 3-7.

Listing 3-7. Binding Constants

```
bindConstant().annotatedWith(…).to(…);
```

Did I forget to specify a type or what? It's kind of hard to explain; you can see the constants you bind as Guice's last hope. If it can't find an exact binding for an injection point that specifies both a type *and* an annotation, it will start looking to see if it can use or convert a constant bound to the same annotation to the desired type. That's why you don't specify a type and why the annotation is *mandatory*.

The `to(...)` method takes either a primitive value (e.g., `char`), a `String`, an `Enum` or a `Class`. Guice provides automated conversion for some of these values. Table 3-1 sums up the conversions that are present in Guice 1.0.

Table 3-1. Constant Conversions Performed by Guice

BINDING	DESTINATION
Primitive (e.g., `int`)	Corresponding primitive wrapper (e.g., `Integer`)
Primitive wrapper	Corresponding primitive
String	Primitive
String	Primitive wrapper
String	Class
String	Enum

Note that, although all the type conversions in Table 3-1 are for immutable types, nothing in Guice forces you to make your injected constants final. So, technically speaking, this feature has little to do with binding constants. By the way, `String` obviously has no corresponding primitive type, so remember that you can't bind an `int` value and inject it into a `String` field.

Now, let's take a look at some examples. Consider the `ConcertHall` class in Listing 3-8.

Listing 3-8. ConcertHall

```
public class ConcertHall {
    @Inject @Named("capacity")
    private int capacity;

    public String toString() {
        return String.format("%s[capacity=%s]",
                        getClass().getName(), capacity);
    }
}
```

I'll now use `bindConstant()` to bind a capacity. Let's start off by using an `int` value, as shown in Listing 3-9.

Listing 3-9. Running the ConcertHall Example with capacity Bound to an int

```
public class ConcertModule extends AbstractModule {
    protected void configure() {
        bindConstant()
            .annotatedWith(Names.named("capacity"))
            .to(322);
    }
}

public class ConcertExample {
    public static void main(String[] args) {
        Injector i = Guice.createInjector(new ConcertModule());
        ConcertHall hall = i.getInstance(ConcertHall.class);
        System.out.println(hall);
    }
}
```

Running this example prints chapter3.constants.ConcertHall[capacity=322] on the console. At this point, no conversion was needed, because we used an `int` value for both locations. Let's try its wrapper type, `Integer`, in Listing 3-10.

Listing 3-10. ConcertHall with Integer capacity

```
public class ConcertHall {
    @Inject @Named("capacity")
    private Integer capacity;

    public String toString() {
        return String.format("%s[capacity=%s]",
                            getClass().getName(), capacity);
    }
}
```

If you run this example, you'll see that it still prints out the same value: chapter3.constants.ConcertHall[capacity=322]. Not surprisingly, you could turn the current binding to injection point int-to-Integer conversion around to be an Integer-to-int conversion.

Note: Primitive wrapper types (e.g., Integer) are supported using Java's *autoboxing* feature. When Java doesn't find a to(...) overload that takes an Integer or a superclass thereof, it will search for an overload that takes the primitive equivalent, int, and will convert the Integer object to an int value automatically. So technically, this conversion is provided by Java, not by Guice.

You could also bind to a String value, as shown in Listing 3-12.

Listing 3-12. ConcertExample Modified to Use String

```
bindConstant()
    .annotatedWith(Names.named("capacity"))
    .to("322");
```

Again, the same result can be seen on the console: chapter3.constants.ConcertHall[capacity=322].

Binding classes and enums is also an interesting option. So let's add some properties to ConcertHall in Listing 3-13.

Listing 3-13. ConcertHall Additions

```java
public enum Setting {
    INDOOR, OUTDOOR
}

public class BigStage {}

public class ConcertHall {
    @Inject @Named("capacity")
    private int capacity;

    @Inject @Named("stage")
    private Class<?> stageType;

    @Inject @Named("setting")
    private Setting setting;

    public String toString() {
        return String.format("%s[capacity=%s, stageType=%s, setting=%s]",
                             getClass().getName(), capacity, stageType, setting);
    }
}
```

To run the newly modified ConcertHall class, I modify my code to look like Listing 3-14.

Listing 3-14. Full-Featured ConcertModule

```java
public class ConcertModule extends AbstractModule {
    protected void configure() {
        bindConstant()
            .annotatedWith(Names.named("capacity"))
            .to("322");
        bindConstant()
            .annotatedWith(Names.named("stage"))
            .to("chapter3.constants.BigStage");
        bindConstant()
            .annotatedWith(Names.named("setting"))
            .to("INDOOR");
    }
}
```

```
public class ConcertExample {
    public static void main(String[] args) {
        Injector i = Guice.createInjector(new ConcertModule());
        ConcertHall hall = i.getInstance(ConcertHall.class);
        System.out.println(hall);
    }
}
```

On the console, you'll now see chapter3.constants.ConcertHall[capacity=322, stageType=class chapter3.constants.BigStage, setting=INDOOR].

Note: Constant bindings to an Enum or a Class don't require you to specify them as a String. I just want to show off the conversion capabilities.

Binding Generic Types

Because of the way Java implements its generics feature, using type erasure, Guice is not able to bind to a generic class directly. Type erasure basically means that only the Java compiler knows about generic types. Once compiled, all that information is gone—erased, if you will. For example, you can't say List<String>.class, because there is no such class at run time. The obvious drawback of this is that Guice cannot know the correct type parameter for a type at run time; you can't refer to a generified class in your bindings.

Tip: To learn more about generics and type erasure, see Angelika Langer's "Generics FAQ" at http://www.angelikalanger.com/GenericsFAQ/JavaGenericsFAQ.html.

CONSTANT BINDING PITFALL

Be on your guard when using Guice's constant bindings. If, for example, you want to inject a long value, but you've specified an int in your binding, your code will *not* work. Take a look at the following example:

```
public class LongHolder {
    @Inject @Named("long")
    private Long theLong;
}

public class LongModule extends AbstractModule {
    protected void configure() {
        bindConstant()
            .annotatedWith(Names.named("long"))
            .to(123);
    }
}

public class LongHolderExample {
    public static void main(String[] args) {
        Injector i = Guice.createInjector(new LongModule());
        i.getInstance(LongHolder.class);
    }
}
```

Running this code will result in a ConfigurationException, telling you that a binding for the LongHolder class's Long value couldn't be found. What's wrong? Well, I forgot to put an "L" after the value, to tell Java this is a long value, not an int value:

```
bindConstant()
    .annotatedWith(Names.named("long"))
    .to(123L);
```

Now the code works as it should. To avoid this nasty problem altogether, I recommend (where possible) the usage of an explicit binding using Guice's toInstance(...) support, which lets you bind to an instance directly. Using this approach, the compiler simply won't *let* you provide an int.

```
bind(Long.class)
    .annotatedWith(Names.named("long"))
    .toInstance(123L);
```

As you would expect, there's a workaround to this language limitation: using a special wrapper class you *save* the generic type information so that Guice can do its magic. This type wrapper class's functionality, TypeLiteral, is explained in Neal Gafter's blog entry "Super Type Tokens" (http://gafter.blogspot.com/2006/12/super-type-tokens.html), albeit under a different name. To use TypeLiteral, you need to subclass it on the spot.

Listing 3-15 provides an example of how to bind a generic type using TypeLiteral.

Listing 3-15. Injecting Generic Types

```java
public class ListUser {
    @Inject @Named("list") List<String> strings;
    @Inject @Named("list") List<Integer> integers;

    public String toString() {
        return String.format("%s[strings=%s, integers=%s]",
                    getClass().getName(),
                    System.identityHashCode(strings),
                    System.identityHashCode(integers));
    }
}

public class TypeLiteralModule extends AbstractModule {
    protected void configure() {
        bind(new TypeLiteral<List<String>>(){})
            .annotatedWith(Names.named("list"))
            .to(new TypeLiteral<ArrayList<String>>(){});
        bind(new TypeLiteral<List<Integer>>(){})
            .annotatedWith(Names.named("list"))
            .to(new TypeLiteral<ArrayList<Integer>>(){});
    }
}
```

```
public class TypeLiteralExample {
    public static void main(String[] args) {
        Injector i = Guice.createInjector(new TypeLiteralModule());
        System.out.println(i.getInstance(ListUser.class));
    }
}
```

Running this example prints something like the following:

```
chapter3.typeliteral.ListUser[strings=24807938, integers=33208902]
```

You'll definitely agree with me that using TypeLiterals makes your code look like the programmer who wrote it just got run over by a tractor. To improve the situation, I recommend that you use factory methods to simplify your code (thanks to Brian Slesinsky for coming up with this idea). As an example, the configuration code in Listing 3-16 is already much more readable—besides the actual factory methods, that is. But you need to write that code only once.

Listing 3-16. Using Factory Methods for More Readable Code

```
public class TypeLiteralModule extends AbstractModule {
    protected void configure() {
        bind(listOf(String.class))
            .annotatedWith(Names.named("list"))
            .to(arrayListOf(String.class));
        bind(listOf(Integer.class))
            .annotatedWith(Names.named("list"))
            .to(arrayListOf(Integer.class));
    }

    @SuppressWarnings("unchecked")
    static <T> TypeLiteral<List<T>> listOf(final Class<T> parameterType) {
        return (TypeLiteral<List<T>>) TypeLiteral.get(new ParameterizedType() {
            public Type[] getActualTypeArguments(){return new Type[]
{parameterType};}
            public Type getRawType() { return List.class; }
            public Type getOwnerType() { return null; }
        });
    }

    @SuppressWarnings("unchecked")
    static <T> TypeLiteral<ArrayList<T>> arrayListOf(final Class<T> parameterType) {
        return (TypeLiteral<ArrayList<T>>) TypeLiteral.get(new ParameterizedType() {
            public Type[] getActualTypeArguments(){return new Type[]
{parameterType};}
            public Type getRawType() { return ArrayList.class; }
```

```
            public Type getOwnerType() { return null; }
        });
    }
}
```

By the way, you don't need to understand why this works. Create methods for your commonly used types, and off you go. Also, take a look at the example implementation scheduled for inclusion in the upcoming Guice version's issue tracker: http://code.google.com/p/google-guice/issues/detail?id=123.

Tip: In the contrary to generic types, arrays are baked into the Java platform, so you can bind arrays like any other type. For example, if you have a Provider<String[]> implementation called MyProvider, you could do the following: bind(String[].class).toProvider(MyProvider.class).

Properties

It's not always appropriate to have configuration in compiled Java. For example, database connection information is something you'll usually want to externalize. To accommodate this use case, Guice can automatically generate bindings from a Properties object.

On the same class you use to bind to @Named annotations, Names, there's a method called bindProperties(...) to which you pass the Guice binder and an in-memory properties file. Take the file in Listing 3-17 as an example.

Listing 3-17. db.properties

```
db.url = jdbc:mysql://localhost/test
db.driver = com.mysql.jdbc.Driver
db.user = test
db.password = test
```

Using the Names.bindProperties(...) method, you can let Guice create @Named bindings to the key of the given set of properties. You *do* need to write your own I/O code, which I think should have been in core Guice. Until then, it's not too hard to write it yourself, like I did for Listing 3-18.

Listing 3-18. Loading and Using db.properties

```java
public class PropertiesModule extends AbstractModule {
    protected void configure() {
        try {
            Properties databaseProperties = loadProperties("db.properties");
            Names.bindProperties(binder(), databaseProperties);
        } catch (RuntimeException e) {
            addError("Could not configure database properties", e);
        }
    }

    private static Properties loadProperties(String name) {
        Properties properties = new Properties();
        InputStream is = new Object(){}
                            .getClass()
                            .getEnclosingClass()
                            .getResourceAsStream(name);
        try {
            properties.load(is);
        } catch(IOException e) {
            throw new RuntimeException(e);
        } finally {
            if (is != null) {
                try {
                    is.close();
                } catch (IOException dontCare) {}
            }
        }
        return properties;
    }
}

public class PropertiesExample {
    @Inject
    public void databaseURL(@Named("db.url") String url) {
        System.out.println(url);
    }

    public static void main(String[] args) {
        Injector i = Guice.createInjector(new PropertiesModule());
        i.getInstance(PropertiesExample.class);
    }
}
```

Running this example prints jdbc:mysql://localhost/test.

Tip: If you should encounter an error in your module configuration, for example, if a properties file could not be found, use `binder.addError(...)` to record the exception. Not throwing exceptions directly lets Guice collect other possible configuration errors so that it can present you with a complete set of errors instead of only the first one.

Static Injection

Although Guice encourages you to minimize the use of static methods or fields through its dependency injection capabilities; sometimes, there's the need to inject them. Listing 3-19 shows how you can make use of static methods while still taking advantage of Guice.

Listing 3-19. Using Static Injection

```
public class StaticModule extends AbstractModule {
    protected void configure() {
        bindConstant().annotatedWith(Names.named("s")).to("D'OH!");
        requestStaticInjection(StaticInjection.class);
    }
}

public class StaticInjection {
    @Inject
    public static void staticMethod(@Named("s") String str) {
        System.out.println(str);
    }

    public static void main(String[] args) {
        Guice.createInjector(new StaticModule());
    }
}
```

Guice injects the classes marked for static injection right before the `Injector` instance returns from creation, so there's no need to call `getInstance(...)` on `Injector`. As you would expect, running this example prints `D'OH!` on the console.

Custom Scopes

In the previous chapter, I demonstrated the singleton scope. To explain how scopes work, I'm going to create an implementation of the default scope, which, in essence, is not a scope because it just creates one new instance per injection request. To implement a scope, you need to implement the Scope interface, which is, in Guice tradition, a simple single-method interface (see Listing 3-20).

Listing 3-20. The Scope Interface

```
public interface Scope {
  <T> Provider<T> scope(Key<T> key, Provider<T> unscoped);
  String toString();
}
```

No wait—Listing 3-20 doesn't only define a single method; it defines toString() too. The Guice authors would really like you to define toString() on your custom scopes, so they put it in so that they could define that contract in the JavaDoc. Anyway, the scope(...) method is of most interest to us, so let's see what it's supposed to do.

Looking at the JavaDoc, you see that the Key argument is the key of the instance being provided, and the Provider is an unscoped provider for that Key that gives out instances from an existing implicit or explicit binding. Guice will call your scope(...) method implementation, so it's up to you how to process that. As a return value, you should return a Provider instance that gives out scoped objects. A typical usage would be to store the actual scoped instances by Key and, if an instance is not already in the store (a Map, persistent storage, and so on), to create an instance using the Provider Guice gave you. You can take a look at the existing Scopes.SINGLETON implementation that ships with Guice if you want to see a realistic example. For now, I'm going with the simplest possible example; the default scope shown in Listing 3-21.

Listing 3-21. Default Scope

```java
public class CustomScopes {
    public static final Scope DEFAULT = new Scope() {
        public <T> Provider<T> scope(Key<T> key, Provider<T> creator) {
            System.out.println("Scoping "+key);
            return creator;
        }
        public String toString() {
            return CustomScopes.class.getSimpleName()+".DEFAULT";
        }
    };
}
```

To use it, you can bind directly to the instance. In Listing 3-22, I'll use it to scope instances of the Person class. As we all know, every person is unique.

Listing 3-22. Binding to the Scope Instance Directly

```java
public class Person {
    public Person() {
        System.out.printf("Hi, I'm a Person. With hashCode '%s', I'm unique!%n",
                          super.hashCode());
    }
}

public class CustomScopeModule extends AbstractModule {
    protected void configure() {
        bind(Person.class).in(CustomScopes.DEFAULT);
    }
}

public class UseCustomScope {
    public static void main(String[] args) {
        Injector i = Guice.createInjector(new CustomScopeModule());
        i.getInstance(Person.class);
        i.getInstance(Person.class);
    }
}
```

This prints something like the following, proving that it actually returns two distinct instances:

```
Scoping Key[type=chapter3.scopes.Person, annotation=[none]]
Hi, I'm a Person. With hashCode '7841785', I'm unique!
Hi, I'm a Person. With hashCode '13141056', I'm unique!
```

Binding directly to the Scope instance works, but there's another option that's actually more flexible. It's also possible to bind to a scope *annotation*. This means that you'd create an annotation to go with the scope and then tell Guice, "Wherever bindings are made to this scope annotation, use the Scope instance I provide here." This extra abstraction has the advantage that you can easily switch entire modules to use another scope by simply changing the implementation to which the scope annotation points. As an extra, you can also tag classes with the scope annotation and get rid of scoping code in your module altogether. But as with @ImplementedBy, you'd probably use that functionality to provide a default scope if none was configured in a module.

Caution: You currently can't use a scope annotation next to @ImplementedBy or @ProvidedBy. In such a case, use the scope annotation on the targeted class. Guice will not—repeat, not—produce an error if you get this wrong.

Anyway, first I need a scope annotation. To make it stand out of the annotation crowd, Guice prescribes me to annotate it with the @ScopeAnnotation annotation, as shown in Listing 3-23.

Listing 3-23. @DefaultScoped

```
@Target(ElementType.TYPE)
@Retention(RetentionPolicy.RUNTIME)
@ScopeAnnotation
public @interface DefaultScoped {}
```

To start using the scope annotation, I now need to link it to the actual Scope implementation, which can be done using the bindScope(...) binder method:

```
bindScope(DefaultScoped.class, CustomScopes.DEFAULT);
```

Now, I can bind to the annotation directly. Note that the order matters: first bind the scope annotation, and only after that, bind objects that use it.

```
bind(Person.class).in(DefaultScoped.class);
```

Listing 3-24 contains the revised example.

Listing 3-24. Binding to a Scope Annotation

```
public class CustomScopeByAnnotationModule extends AbstractModule {
    protected void configure() {
        bindScope(DefaultScoped.class, CustomScopes.DEFAULT);
        bind(Person.class).in(DefaultScoped.class);
    }
}

public class UseCustomScopeByAnnotation {
    public static void main(String[] args) {
        Injector i = Guice.createInjector(new CustomScopeByAnnotationModule());
        i.getInstance(Person.class);
        i.getInstance(Person.class);
    }
}
```

For a confidence boost, I run it again:

```
Scoping Key[type=chapter3.scopes.Person, annotation=[none]]
Hi, I'm a Person. With hashCode '11665455', I'm unique!
Hi, I'm a Person. With hashCode '14800362', I'm unique!
```

Excellent! If I now wanted to use the annotation-driven style, that would be as simple as slapping the annotation on Person. And not unimportantly, a line of configuration can also be deleted, as shown in Listing 3-25.

Listing 3-25. Annotation-Driven Scoping

```
public class CustomScopeByAnnotationModule extends AbstractModule {
    protected void configure() {
        bindScope(DefaultScoped.class, CustomScopes.DEFAULT);
        // yay, less configuration!
    }
}

@DefaultScoped
public class Person {
    public Person() {
        System.out.printf("Hi, I'm a Person. With hashCode '%s', I'm unique!%n",
                          super.hashCode());
    }
}
```

Knowing how scopes work and understanding the differences between the instance and annotation styles will make your Guice configuration better and more flexible.

Tempting as it may be, you will rarely need to implement your own scope. If you need caching, use a cache. If you need a custom Scope, take a look at the existing ones again. The web scopes, for example, often come in handy.

Note: Why not use Scope for caching? Well, it's not that much of a mismatch, but I think there are better options. For example, using AOP to implement caching is much more flexible, powerful, and feels more natural than using a scope. The next chapter explains about AOP and what Guice does in that area.

Web Scopes

Besides the built-in singleton scope (which is *not* used by default, remember), the Guice 1.0 distribution also comes with a couple of web-related scopes: HTTP request and HTTP session. When you use these, your scoped objects will live as long as the HttpServletRequest or the HttpSession, respectively. These scopes obviously make use of the Servlet API and need a web container that implements the Servlet 2.3 specification or above. For all web examples in this book, I will use Jetty, which you can download from the http://www.mortbay.org web site.

The actual bits for the web scopes are inside the guice-servlet-1.0.jar file from the Guice 1.0 distribution, so first, don't forget to add it to the classpath when trying out these scopes. Once you have that, you need to do two things before you can get started:

- Install the ServletModule Module for the Injector you will create.

- Configure the GuiceFilter servlet Filter in your web.xml file to intercept all requests.

ServletModule will install both scopes and create bindings for a number of HTTP-related objects:

- HttpServletRequest

- HttpServletResponse

- HttpSession

- A Map<String, String[]> type annotated with the @RequestParameters binding annotation, containing HttpServletRequest ParameterMap.

To configure GuiceFilter, add something like this to your web.xml file:

```
<filter>
    <filter-name>GuiceFilter</filter-name>
    <filter-class>com.google.inject.servlet.GuiceFilter</filter-class>
</filter>
<filter-mapping>
    <filter-name>GuiceFilter</filter-name>
    <url-pattern>/*</url-pattern>
</filter-mapping>
```

Next, you can scope your classes by using or binding to the @RequestScoped or @SessionScoped scope annotations, or take a look at the ServletScopes class if you wish to bind to the Scope instances directly.

Caution: Be careful when mixing scopes. If a singleton-scoped object keeps a reference to a session-scoped one, you'll end up with strange bugs for sure. As a rule of thumb, never keep a reference in an object that points to an object in a narrower scope. And if you really, really need to do it anyway, you could inject the Provider instance instead and call get() on it only when you're absolutely sure that the requested object is currently in scope. More on this in Chapter 7.

This short introduction actually concludes the raw servlet functionality in Guice 1.0. The next version of Guice will offer better integration with the Web, like infrastructure to manage Injector creation or to inject into servlets. More important is integration with web frameworks, for example, the Struts 2 integration that ships with version 1.0. There will be more on that in Chapter 5.

Organizing Modules

In the "Custom Scopes" section, I showed you how binding to a scope annotation instead of a Scope implementation will add to your Guice application's flexibility. To fully enjoy what that gives you, there are better ways to organize your configuration than putting it all in a single Module implementation. To go back to the same example, you can create two modules so that the Scope registration is easy to reuse. Listing 3-26 shows an example.

Listing 3-26. Scope Registration in a Separate Module

```java
public class DefaultScopeModule extends AbstractModule {
    protected void configure() {
        bindScope(DefaultScoped.class, CustomScopes.DEFAULT);
    }
}

public class BindingsModule extends AbstractModule {
    protected void configure() {
        bind(Person.class).in(DefaultScoped.class);
    }
}

public class UseCustomScopeInModules {
    public static void main(String[] args) {
        Injector i = Guice.createInjector(
            new DefaultScopeModule(),
            new BindingsModule()
        );
        i.getInstance(Person.class);
        i.getInstance(Person.class);
    }
}
```

The code in Listing 3-26 works, but you need to be careful that you register the scope module *before* you register any modules that use it—not to mention that you need to remember to register it. A better option is to define an explicit dependency on the DefaultScopeModule. To do that, use the install method on Binder (or for AstractModule, the delegating method).

Listing 3-27. Using Binder.install(...)

```
public class BindingsModule extends AbstractModule {
    protected void configure() {
        install(new DefaultScopeModule());
        bind(Person.class).in(DefaultScoped.class);
    }
}

public class UseCustomScopeInModules {
    public static void main(String[] args) {
        Injector i = Guice.createInjector(new BindingsModule());
        i.getInstance(Person.class);
        i.getInstance(Person.class);
    }
}
```

To make the latter strategy, shown in Listing 3-27, even more flexible, you can choose to create a top-level *application* Module that does nothing but install other modules. It might sound ridiculous for this small example, but rest assured that this will save you from a whole lot of frowning when working on a larger project. Creating these groups of modules is what makes them such a joy to use. Whatever code you will want to be able to test in isolation, put it in a different module so that it can be swapped out easily. Listing 3-28 shows how this might look for the example at hand.

Listing 3-28. Module Panacea

```
public class ApplicationModule extends AbstractModule {
    protected void configure() {
        install(new DefaultScopeModule());
        install(new BindingsModule());
    }
}

public class UseCustomScopeWithApplicationModule {
    public static void main(String[] args) {
        Injector i = Guice.createInjector(new ApplicationModule());
        i.getInstance(Person.class);
        i.getInstance(Person.class);
    }
}
```

Besides using "testable in isolation" or logical software layers as Module boundaries (service layer, data layer, and so on), you can also choose to use packages as a boundary. A module-per-package strategy will allow you to make all concrete implementation classes package private, which means that users of the API *must* program against the interfaces. Just know that this ties you to Guice. If only *Guice* can reach the implementation, your code is useless without the framework, or at least without any DI framework. Anyway, I'll talk more about these visibility possibilities in Chapter 7.

The Binding EDSL

You've seen that Guice uses a special syntax for its modules that reads as if it were an English sentence. To allow you to participate in a buzzword discussion, here's some of the theory behind it. This "human readable" concept is what you could call an Embedded Domain Specific Language (EDSL). Simply put, it's a small language about DI within the Java language. Bob and company used a concept called Fluent Interfaces (http://martinfowler.com/bliki/ FluentInterface.html) to implement this, which is a fluent method chaining style of API to keep your configuration simple, readable, and maintainable. For this book's Appendix, I prepared a simplified example of how you would implement this yourself, in case you're interested.

Now, this section is *really* about a final review of what the Binding EDSL can do. I'll do this by example; to save some trees, I'll use the AbstractModule syntax, thus omitting binder. at the start of each example. Take it away!

```
bind(Implementation.class);
```

This explicitly binds the Implementation class to itself. Because Guice already knows how to handle simple concrete classes, it's not needed to define bindings that look like the preceding example. It's more likely that you'll use something like the following:

```
bind(Interface.class).to(Implementation.class);
```

Using this, you specify that all requests, be they injection requests or explicit requests using the Injector, will return an Implementation class wherever an object of the Interface type is requested. Remember that bindings in modules always take precedence: this will override annotation-style configuration like `@ImplementedBy` or `@ProvidedBy`.

```
bind(Interface.class).toProvider(InterfaceProvider.class);
```

Much like the previous example, this one also defines what will be returned for each `Interface` request, but this time, we're using a binding to a `Provider<Interface>` implementation. Guice will inject the return value of the `InterfaceProvider.get()` method wherever an `Interface` instance is requested. Providers don't *need* to return a new instance each time, but it's a good idea for them to do so. If you want to control instance lifetime, use scopes instead:

```
bind(Interface.class).annotatedWith(Guicy.class).to(Implementation.class);
```

The preceding example is very similar to the second example, but here, I also specify an annotation to bind to. Remember that Guice internally identifies bindings by `Key`, which is a combination of a type (`Interface.class`) and an optional annotation type (`Guicy.class`). This binding will match all the combinations of `Interface` and `Guicy`, including occurrences in which `Guicy` holds a value. It matches on both *types* and nothing else. If you would like to match on more than the annotation *type*, consider using `@Named` or implement similar functionality using your own annotation type:

```
bind(Implementation.class).in(Singleton.class);
// or, alternatively:
bind(Implementation.class).in(Scopes.SINGLETON);
```

Both of the preceding bindings bind the `Implementation` type in the singleton scope: on the first line by binding to the binding annotation and on the second line by binding to the `Scope` instance directly. This means that Guice will only create one instance of `Implementation` per `Injector` *and* per `Key`. You are defining singleton scope *only for this binding*, and thus *only this* `Key`. Other bindings to `Implementation` that define a binding annotation will not be singleton scoped unless you define them as such. And if you do, Guide will create two different instances. Again, this binding overrides any scope annotations on the classes themselves. To make sure a singleton loads eagerly no matter what the `Injector`'s Stage is, use `bind(Implementation.class).asEagerSingleton()`:

```
bind(new TypeLiteral<Interface<String>>(){}).to(StringImplementation.class);
```

This awful-looking code is the only way to bind a parameterized type. For all `Interface<String>` requests, a `StringImplementation` will be returned. If you forget to use `TypeLiteral`, the binding would match all the `Interface` requests, not only the `Interface<String>` ones:

```
bind(Interface.class).toInstance(new Implementation());
```

In this example, you instantly provide an instance in your `Module` configuration, thus you don't allow Guice to construct `Implementation` or to inject into the constructor. Guice will, however, perform field and setter injection on the instance when the `Injector` is first created.

Tip: Using `toInstance(...)` is usually a bad idea, the exception being constant bindings. First, it locks in the scope of the binding, because you provide an instance directly. Second, you would be mixing application logic with configuration. Third, you can't use constructor injection, which makes it harder to ensure that instances are immutable and thread safe. Avoid the temptation, and consider using an eager singleton instead.

By the way, it *is* possible to inject into objects yourself, after they have been constructed. To perform such after-the-fact injection on fields and setters, use the `Injector`'s `injectMembers(Object)` method:

```
injector.injectMembers(someObject);
```

Anyway, let's go back to the Binding EDSL for a final example.

```
bindConstant().annotatedWith(Names.named("one")).to("1");
```

The preceding line sets up a constant binding. Constant bindings don't have a type defined, and therefore, the binding annotation is mandatory. These bindings are Guice's last hope. When no binding to a given type and annotation is found, Guice will start looking at the constant bindings with the same binding annotation type and will, for a limited set of types, try to convert a matching constant binding's type to the desired one if needed.

Because a lot of its examples can be combined, this section doesn't cover all of the Binding EDSL's possibilities. You don't need to know it all by heart anyway; most IDEs have decent code completion to assist you while defining your bindings.

One last interesting thing to note is that the `Injector` has several bindings configured by default. The resulting instances are injectable, even in `Providers` (but *not* in `Scope` instances, which are not managed). So yes, you can inject the `Injector`—if you're sure that you don't just need one or more providers, that is. When you're done frowning, here's the rundown of the default bindings:

- The `Injector`
- A `Provider<T>` instance for all types, even for the ones not bound to a `Provider`
- The JDK `Logger` instance for the class being injected
- The `Stage` constant defining the stage in which the `Injector` was created

How Guice Resolves Dependencies

You may never need to know this, but when you're debugging a Guice problem, you can come back to this section to make sure that your understanding about the injection flow is correct. Perhaps it's *not* a Guice problem; you never know. Roughly the following events will happen when trying to fulfill an injection request transitively:

1. Arrive at an injection point, and get the type of the injection point and its binding annotation, if present. Next, for this key, try to find a binding. If there is one, use it to create an instance, either directly or using a bound `Provider<T>` or instance.
2. If no exact binding is available, go over the constant bindings to see if a conversion is possible for constant bindings to the same annotation type.
3. If the injection point used an annotation type or value, produce an error now.
4. Otherwise, examine the type: look for `@ImplementedBy` or `@ProvidedBy`, and if present, use it to locate an instance.
5. Try to create the type itself.

6. There are no options left; Guice can't get the instance and will produce an error.

Tip: Guice supports circular dependencies for all bindings that bind to an interface.

Summary

If your Guice knowledge were like a movie, you'd now be horribly close to looking at hundreds of police cars while Bruce Willis kisses some girl. But before you move on to the last topic there is to know about core Guice, AOP, here's a quick summary of what you put yourself through in this chapter. You've now learned that

- Providers help you deal with legacy code, third-party APIs, the multiple instances problem, and delayed construction.
- @Named helps you get started quickly without having to create binding annotations.
- Constant bindings are shorthand for defining simple values; they perform magical conversions, and they are Guice's *last hope* for annotated injection points.
- Binding to generic types requires you to use an awkward syntax involving the TypeLiteral class.
- Guice can create @Named bindings for you from a set of properties.
- It's possible to inject static members.
- Scopes are a simple but powerful concept.
- There are web scopes for HTTP session and HTTP request.
- Organizing modules can be real fun if you do it right.
- The Binding EDSL is expensive talk for something that's dead simple.

- You don't need to care much about how dependency resolution happens.
- You still don't seem to need any XML.

Chapter 4: Aspect-Oriented Programming

Aspect-Oriented Programming, commonly abbreviated as AOP, is a concept that will save you from copying and pasting the same lines of (boilerplate) code over and over again. Follow me in my reasoning:

- Transaction handling code is everywhere in the code.

- Because transaction handling code is everywhere, there is more code.

- Because there is more code, there are more bugs.

- You miss the deadline, because there are too many bugs.

- You need to work overtime at the office, because you missed the deadline.

- Your firstborn said her first words while you were at the office.

Even if you're not familiar with AOP, you know what I mean. Object-oriented languages like Java have concepts to micromanage modularization. You have been using classes, methods, and packages for years, but these concepts don't solve all problems: they can't always help you organize your code so that it contains as little duplication as possible. You want to be able to add to, change, or remove program behavior globally. Examples of these cross-cutting concerns are transaction handling, logging, security, and exception handling. Wherever you see similar code scattered throughout the code base that does not contribute to the actual business logic, that code is a possible target for AOP. Likewise, when you want to manipulate existing program functionality in a programwide fashion, AOP may help you out. For example, you sometimes want to make the following statements a reality: "Access to all the service classes needs to be logged." Or, "All DAO methods need to be transactional." You can do things like *that* with Guice AOP, as you'll see in this chapter.

Note: This chapter is written for people new to Guice AOP and AOP in general.

AOP for Mere Mortals

As you would expect, Guice AOP stands on the shoulders of giants. The most notable project in the area is probably AspectJ (http://eclipse.org/aspectj) from the Eclipse Foundation; it has pioneered many AOP concepts we know today and is one of the most feature-complete AOP implementations in existence. Also notable is the Spring Framework (http://www.springframework.org), which has brought DI and AOP into the mainstream. Last but not least, it's comforting to know that Bob Lee, Guice's creator, is quite the AOP expert himself. He created some of the early AOP implementations for Java like JAdvise and Dynaop (https://dynaop.dev.java.net/), and cofounded the AOP Alliance project, which produces a standard AOP API on which Spring and, unsurprisingly, Guice build.

That said, though AOP solves a good number of problems, there still are issues—the most important being that most current implementations are too difficult to use. There's a whole set of terminology and even a minilanguage to learn, and often, you need to change your build process to include an extra compile step so that the AOP functionality can do its work.

Guice is different in that it acknowledges that you use 20 percent of AOP features 80 percent of the time. By implementing only the most important set of functionality and dropping a lot of the expensive terminology, Guice's AOP is elegant, easy to use, and powerful, and it has zero impact on your development process. It's what I like to call "AOP for mere mortals." You don't need a PhD to use it.

How Guice AOP Works

AOP is usually about doing work before or after (or both) a piece of code executes in your application. To be able to do that without modifying your code, Guice AOP generates proxies (impersonators, if you will) for your targeted objects. For example, let's say you want to print every method that gets called on YourObject to the console. To achieve this, Guice *impersonates* YourObject with a proxy instance and first routes all incoming method invocations to YourObject through code that, in this example, prints them to the console. These layers of code between the impersonator and the actual instance are called interceptors. Figure 4-1 illustrates this concept.

Figure 4-1. A conceptual view of Guice AOP

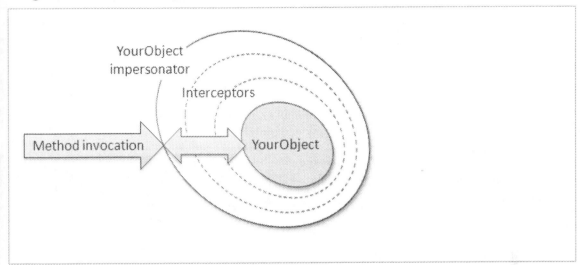

Although some AOP frameworks do even more magic involving special-purpose compilers and code rewriting, Guice AOP is *all about intercepting method calls*, using the simple mechanism described in Figure 4-1. So enough talk about Guice's code, let's take a look at how *your* code will look.

Caution: Because Guice AOP, or any other AOP framework for that matter, impersonates objects by using proxy instances, you should watch out when using reference equality checks (==) in your code. When you compare a *real* instance with a proxy instance, you will see incorrect results!

Method Interception

As you would expect, Guice AOP makes use of the same configuration concepts I introduced earlier in the book. In addition to all the other bindXXX methods that you have already used in your module configuration, there's also the one shown in Listing 4-1.

Listing 4-1. Guice AOP in Three Lines of Code

```
void bindInterceptor(Matcher<? super Class<?>> classMatcher,
                     Matcher<? super Method> methodMatcher,
                     MethodInterceptor... interceptors) {…}
```

First, you pass in two Matcher objects: one to match on classes and one to match on those classes' methods. For that combination, you can specify zero or more method interceptors of the MethodInterceptor type, not that specifying zero interceptors makes any sense.

This MethodInterceptor interface, shown in Listing 4-2, is the thing Guice will call whenever a matching method is invoked. It's just a simple interface that you need to implement.

Listing 4-2. MethodInterceptor

```
public interface MethodInterceptor extends Interceptor {
    Object invoke(MethodInvocation invocation) throws Throwable;
}
```

Tip: Always use matchers to match classes and methods; avoid doing your own filtering in your MethodInterceptor. Doing your own filtering will affect performance, because matchers run only once at startup, while interceptors get invoked every time they intercept a method call.

Guice will call the invoke method with an appropriate MethodInvocation object for all intercepted method invocations. This MethodInvocation instance is the object that puts you in the driver's seat; by executing invocation.proceed(), you'll call the original intercepted method, and you'll get the return value if there is one. This mechanism allows you to do several things, depending on the method:

- Execute code before the intercepted method executes.

- Call the intercepted method with slightly or entirely different parameters.

- Execute code after the intercepted method executes.

- Postprocess the return value or return anything of your liking.

- Don't call the method at all, or call a different method.

The original caller will get the return value that *you* return from the invoke method, so make sure to return either `invocation.proceed()` or the value you prefer.

Note: Next to scopes, method interceptors are the only important Guice artifact that you can't inject into in Guice 1.0. Workarounds are possible though; for more information, see http://tembrel.blogspot.com/2007/09/injecting-method-interceptors-in-guice.html.

As for the `Matcher` instances, most `Matcher` classes that you'll ever need ship with Guice and can be found in the `Matchers` class. Table 4-1 explains the `Matchers` methods in Guice 1.0.

Table 4-1. Methods on the Matchers Class in Guice 1.0

MATCHER	DESCRIPTION	APPLICABILITY
`any()`	Match anything.	Classes and methods
`not(...)`	Invert another `Matcher`.	Classes and methods
`annotatedWith(...)`	Match an annotation.	Classes and methods
`subclassesOf(...)`	Match the given class and its subclasses.	Classes
`only(...)`	Match on equality using `equals`.	Classes and methods
`identicalTo(...)`	Match on reference equality (`==`).	Classes and methods
`inPackage(...)`	Match all classes in the given package.	Classes
`returns(...)`	Match method return type.	Methods

Before I move on to the code, let me mention a few facts you should be aware of. Using the matchers shown in Table 4-1, Guice AOP can *match only objects created by Guice*. So yes, this rules out Guice AOP when using after-the-fact injection like `toInstance(...)`, `injectMembers(...)` or `requestStaticInjection(...)`. However, Guice *does* match on the following:

- Concrete classes that were specified in the `to(...)` method of your bindings.
- Concrete classes made available by an implicit binding.

This means that although you can match all the objects that Guice creates, you can not match on abstract classes, interfaces, or any of their methods. At least not directly you can't; for example, `subclassesOf(...)` does work.

Theory aside, Guice AOP will become clear once you've seen an example. Throw `aopalliance.jar` in the classpath, and off we go.

Phoning Home

Did you ever wonder if someone is tapping your phone? You know, maybe the FBI guys staking out the front of your house—too bad they're in an ice cream truck and it's snowing outside. That's what happens when all the senior guys get desk jobs.

So, it's a beautiful Sunday, and you feel like calling Aunt Jane. First, you need a phone, and you need Jane to receive your call on the other end. Listing 4-3 shows what the calling process could look like.

Listing 4-3. Phone Call Prerequisites

```java
public class Phone {
    private static final Map<Number, Receiver> RECEIVERS =
        new HashMap<Number, Receiver>();

    static {
        RECEIVERS.put(123456789, new Receiver("Aunt Jane"));
    }

    public Receiver call(Number number) {
        return RECEIVERS.get(number);
    }
}

public class Receiver {
    private final String name;
    public Receiver(String name) {
        this.name = name;
    }
    public String toString() {
        return String.format("%s[name=%s]", getClass().getName(), name);
    }
}
```

When the phone company person came at your house and installed your phone
(see Listing 4-4), little did you know that the technician was actually from the
FBI!

Listing 4-4. The Phone Company's Installation

```java
import static com.google.inject.matcher.Matchers.*;

public class PhoneModule extends AbstractModule {
    protected void configure() {
        bindInterceptor(
            subclassesOf(Phone.class),
            returns(only(Receiver.class)),
            new PhoneLoggerInterceptor()
        );
    }
}
```

```java
public class MakePhoneCall {
    public static void main(String[] args) {
        Injector i = Guice.createInjector(new PhoneModule());
    }
}
```

Son of a gun—the technician installed a phone call logger! By the way, notice that import static was used on the Matchers class; that's why you don't see it anywhere. The FBI's coders know Java 5; you have to give them that. Anyway, in plain English, it matches code with the following characteristics: "Phone or something like Phone where the method(s) return Receiver." That finds a match in the call method in Phone:

```java
public Receiver call(Number number) {
    return RECEIVERS.get(number);
}
```

It looks like switching your Phone is not going to help, as long as you're using something like a Phone with methods that return a Receiver. Those are definitely not your average ice cream truck operators. Listing 4-5 shows how their logging system works.

Listing 4-5. The Phone Call Logger

```java
public class PhoneLoggerInterceptor implements MethodInterceptor {
    public Object invoke(MethodInvocation invocation) throws Throwable {
        for (Object arg : invocation.getArguments())
            if (arg instanceof Number)
                System.out.println("CALL: "+arg);

        return invocation.proceed();
    }
}
```

They iterate over all the method arguments, and if one of them is Number, they log it. Next, they simply let the phone call proceed. Let's see what happens if you call Aunt Jane (see Listing 4-6).

Listing 4-6. Calling Aunt Jane

```java
public class MakePhoneCall {
    public static void main(String[] args) {
        Injector i = Guice.createInjector(new PhoneModule());
        Phone phone = i.getInstance(Phone.class);
        Receiver auntJane = phone.call(123456789);
    }
}
```

That looks like a regular phone call to me. But if you run this, it prints CALL: 123456789. Yep, the FBI agents suck up all the numbers you call. Listing 4-7 shows what else they could have done.

Listing 4-7. Phone Call Redirection

```java
public class PhoneRedirectInterceptor implements MethodInterceptor {
    public Object invoke(MethodInvocation invocation) throws Throwable {
        return new Receiver("Alberto's Pizza Place");
    }
}
```

Now, install this interceptor as shown in Listing 4-8, and see what happens.

Listing 4-8. Adding PhoneCallRedirect

```java
public class PhoneModule extends AbstractModule {
    protected void configure() {
        bindInterceptor(
            subclassesOf(Phone.class),
            returns(only(Receiver.class)),
            new PhoneLoggerInterceptor(),
            new PhoneRedirectInterceptor()
        );
    }
}
```

If you now call Aunt Jane again, some woman asks if you, "Wanta bigga pizza?" Just when you thought Aunt Jane was on a diet!

Listing 4-9. Calling Aunt Jane Again?

```java
public class MakePhoneCall {
    public static void main(String[] args) {
        Injector i = Guice.createInjector(new PhoneModule());
        Phone phone = i.getInstance(Phone.class);
        Receiver auntJane = phone.call(123456789);
```

```
        System.out.println(auntJane);
    }
}
```

If you run the code in Listing 4-9, it prints the following:

```
CALL: 123456789
chapter4.Receiver[name=Alberto's Pizza Place]
```

You see that the logger is still in place, but now, the Receiver is Alberto's **Pizza** Place.

By the way, did you notice how easy it is to reuse and apply method interceptors? That's an interesting reuse case. The FBI agents only need to write the method interceptor once, and then it can be applied to all the phones in the world—the powah!

Tip: As you can see in the phone call example, the interceptors were applied in the order in which they appeared in the module. This is something you can safely depend on. The execution order is determined by the order in which modules appear at Injector creation, by the bindInterceptor(...) call order, and by the bindInterceptor(...) argument order. However, if you're seriously depending on the order in which your interceptors are applied, it's best to define them in the same module to make that clear.

Summary

Knowing and using AOP will make you feel like a secret agent. By limiting itself to method interception, Guice AOP shines in its simplicity. It's child's play to install and use a MethodInterceptor, and it will save you from typing the same code over and over again. To successfully return from an AOP mission, here's what you need to do:

- Use the Matchers class to match specific classes or methods.

- Use binder.bindInterceptor in a Module to point MethodInterceptor instances to all the matches.

- Remember that Guice AOP only works for objects Guice creates!

That is all, special agent Duke. This chapter will self-destruct in 5 seconds.

Chapter 5: Integrating with the Web

All the code examples in the previous chapters had to be run from a main method or a test case. However, it would be foolish to assume that most people write applications that are that simple. Most applications that I, and probably you, write are ultimately web applications, whether you work on the front end or not. On the Java platform, that usually means directly using servlet technology (http://java.sun.com/products/servlet/) or using it indirectly through an MVC framework like Struts (http://struts.apache.org). In this chapter, I will discuss both options from the ground up.

The Integration Challenge

As you probably know, a web container like Tomcat or Jetty has what you could call a *managed environment*. By using the Servlet API and delivering your application in a certain format (e.g., as a WAR file), you get some things for free, like HTTP abstraction, life cycle callbacks, filters, simple state management, and threading.

Because you'll want to minimize the dependency on an actual DI framework, you'll want to start injection at the highest possible level, which is the servlet layer in this case. But the servlet layer's managed nature brings some challenges to the table:

- *Bootstrapping*: The container handles application start-up; you need some way to bootstrap the DI framework early in execution, before you get any user requests.

- *Servlets are not in the club*: HttpServlet objects, or Filter objects for that matter, get created by the web container, which rules out constructor injection, AOP, and scoping.

While Guice 1.0 ships with servlet *scopes*, it does not ship with any direct DI integration for the Web (besides the Struts 2 plug-in, which I'll discuss later). The upcoming sections are largely based on the solution that will probably make it into the next Guice release.

Bootstrapping

Hooking into application start-up is the first issue that needs solving. People starting out with Guice often run into this problem. After looking at the simplest of code examples, which all run from a main method, they're lost when they want to use Guice in an environment with no main available. The servlet environment is a good example of this.

Luckily, since the Servlet 2.3 specification, a *listener* mechanism is in place. By implementing an API interface and adding the resulting listener class to web.xml, the container will notify your code of application events like session creation or application start-up, depending on which interfaces you chose to implement. Because we're obviously interested in application start-up, we'll need to use the interface shown in Listing 5-1, called ServletContextListener, which is able to receive application start-up and shutdown events.

Listing 5-1. The javax.servlet.ServletContextListener Interface

```
public interface ServletContextListener
    void contextDestroyed(ServletContextEvent sce);
    void contextInitialized(ServletContextEvent sce);
}
```

The ServletContextListener mechanism is as high up the stack as we'll ever get to create the Injector. To make it available in the application, the obvious choice is to store it in the ServletContext, which holds the applicationwide state for a web application. You can see an example implementation of this concept in Listing 5-2.

Listing 5-2. A Guice ServletContextListener Approach

```
public class GuiceServletContextListener implements ServletContextListener {
    public static final String KEY = Injector.class.getName();

    public void contextInitialized(ServletContextEvent sce) {
      sce.getServletContext().setAttribute(KEY, getInjector());
    }

    public void contextDestroyed(ServletContextEvent sce) {
      sce.getServletContext().removeAttribute(KEY);
    }
```

```
    private Injector getInjector() {
        // return the application's injector
    }
}
```

Having the `Injector` available at start-up is one thing, but how do servlets get injected now? Let's see about that next.

Inviting Servlets to the Club

The easiest way to inject a servlet is to override its `init(...)` method and use `Injector.injectMembers(Object)`. This `init(...)` method will get called right after the instance is created by the container. After that, Guice's `injectMembers(...)` feature comes in handy; it can inject the servlet's fields and methods marked with `@Inject`. Listing 5-3 shows how that looks.

Listing 5-3. Injecting javax.servlet.http.HttpServlet

```
public class SomeServlet extends HttpServlet {
    @Override
    public void init(ServletConfig config) throws ServletException {
        super.init(config);
        ServletContext servletContext = config.getServletContext();
        Injector injector =
            (Injector) servletContext.getAttribute(GuiceServletContextListener.KEY);
        injector.injectMembers(this);
    }

    // override other methods like doGet, doPost
}
```

For better reuse, you'll want to create a base `HttpServlet` class so that you don't have to write the same `init(...)` code over and over again.

Tip: In the current Guice Subversion repository, you'll find reference implementations for both classes I discussed, called `GuiceServletContextListener` and `InjectedHttpServlet` respectively. If you're using Guice 1.0 and need raw servlet functionality, I suggest you download them there. Just go to http://code.google.com/p/google-guice/source, and search for the class names.

You'll find a full Hello Servlet Guice example demonstrating servlet injection in the appendix of this book.

Configuration Discovery

A question that often comes up is how you should dynamically discover `Module` implementations, instead of hard-coding them in a `ServletContextListener` or something similar. Because this means different things to different people, I'm going to break up the whole question into three categories. Then, I'll give you my recommendations on how to handle them.

- *Integration test independence*: You don't have the module you need at compile time, because you want to test only one application layer in isolation.

- *Automated discovery*: You want to be able to drop in a JAR file and pick up its modules automatically at application start-up.

- *Everything more advanced*: You need to perform tasks that don't fall into the previous two categories, like reloading a graph of objects at runtime if configuration changes.

In the first case, you probably need to rethink how you build applications using modules. This doesn't even have much to do with dynamic discovery—you should simply consider creating the `Injector` with a different set of `Modules` altogether. For example, if you have a `DatabaseLayerModule` class, you might want to create the injector with a `MockDatabaseLayerModule` module when integration testing other parts of the application.

The second category is a different story. First, it's worth noting that JDK 6 does have an out-of-the-box solution: `java.util.ServiceLoader`. I highly recommend that you read the JavaDoc for that class. In this second category, I would also put simplest of templating approaches, where you want to specify a root `Module` name but don't want have it available at compile time. You can easily solve this by using, for example, a `<context-param>` with the root `Module` class name for your application and then get an instance of that `Module` using reflection when creating the `Injector`. This is not rocket science and might fit your needs if you're not on JDK 6. Listing 5-4 shows an example implementation.

Listing 5-4. Quick and Dirty Templating Example

```
<!-- web.xml -->
<web-app>
    ...
    <context-param>
      <param-name>module</param-name>
      <param-value>discovery.HelloGuiceModule</param-value>
      <description>Guice Module to load on startup</description>
    </context-param>
    ...
</web-app>

// GuiceServletContextListener class
public class GuiceServletContextListener implements ServletContextListener {
    public static final String KEY = Injector.class.getName();

    public void contextInitialized(ServletContextEvent sce) {
        sce.getServletContext()
            .setAttribute(KEY, getInjector(sce.getServletContext()));
    }

    public void contextDestroyed(ServletContextEvent sce) {
        sce.getServletContext().removeAttribute(KEY);
    }

    private Injector getInjector(ServletContext ctx) {
        String fqClassName = ctx.getInitParameter("module");
        try {
            @SuppressWarnings("unchecked")
            Class<? extends Module> module =
                (Class<? extends Module>) Class.forName(fqClassName);
            return Guice.createInjector(module.getConstructor().newInstance());
        } catch (Exception e) {
            throw new RuntimeException(e);
        }
    }
}
```

As for the third and last category, consider using an advanced component model like OSGi (http://www.osgi.org). There's a project called Peaberry available that is working on OSGi integration for Guice; it can be found at http://code.google.com/p/peaberry/. This integration is still at a very early stage, so it probably makes more sense to use the Spring Framework if you have a hard dependency on this kind of functionality. It has the best OSGi integration I've seen so far.

Now, all this grunt work aside, you're probably better off opting for an MVC framework that offers Guice integration. Solid framework integration allows you to forget most of the things I just talked about.

Struts 2

As I briefly mentioned in Chapter 2, Guice 1.0 ships with a plug-in for Struts 2 (http://struts.apache.org), the successor to the very popular Struts MVC framework. That said, don't use the plug-in version that ships with Guice 1.0; it is horribly broken. Go to the Guice project web site and get version 1.0.1 (guice-struts2-plugin-1.0.1.jar), which is available as a separate download.

Using the Struts 2 plug-in, you can inject your Struts actions, interceptors, and any other classes you use. Scopes currently work everywhere except with interceptors. What's interesting about Struts 2 is that the framework was designed with DI in mind from the beginning. If its designers hadn't done that, they would have ended up with something like the basic servlet integration I mentioned earlier, where you can only use after-the-fact injection like injectMembers(...) for your web artifacts, simply because you don't control object creation. This means that only the objects lower down the stack, starting at the ones that get injected using injectMembers(...), can benefit from some key DI advantages: constructor injection, scopes, and AOP. When using Struts 2, you don't have that problem: Guice can control the full object life cycle.

Note: Technically speaking, Struts 2 is DI friendly because of its use of the XWork 2 framework (http://www.opensymphony.com/xwork/), which, interestingly enough, uses an early version of Guice internally. Take a look at the com.opensymphony.xwork2.inject package in the XWork API, and notice the similarities.

To use Guice with Struts 2, you generally need to do the following:

1. Set up Struts 2 (`http://struts.apache.org/2.x/docs/bootstrap.html`).

2. Make the Guice plug-in (and Guice) available in `WEB-INF/lib` of your application.

3. Configure your `struts.xml` file to use Guice's `ObjectFactory`; apparently, you don't always need this, but better safe than sorry: `<constant name="struts.objectFactory" value="guice" />`

4. Optionally (you could also use annotations only), specify the root module in `struts.xml`: `<constant name="guice.module" value="helloguice.HelloModule"/>`.

By default, the plug-in will create the `Injector` in the default `Stage`, `Stage.DEVELOPMENT`. This is unfortunate and should be fixed in the upcoming version of the plug-in. Mapping the `Stage` one-to-one to the already existing Struts property `struts.devMode` would have made more sense.

Caution: You can't use Struts's custom type converter functionality in the current version of the plug-in (1.0.1). Until the next version ships, there's a fix available on the Guice mailing list. See `http://groups.google.com/group/google-guice/browse_thread/thread/5069bb48c3e0f156`.

This is all the time I'm going to spend on Struts 2 now. In the next chapter, I will discuss an example web application that uses this framework. If you just want a quick example, there's one in the Guice source distribution, which you can download from the Guice project web site.

Caution: The current version of the Struts 2 plug-in (1.0.1) installs Guice's `ServletModule` by default. You can't turn that off, but you are usually going to use it anyway. Just remember *not* to install it in your own modules. You'll still need to configure the `GuiceFilter` for the web scopes to work, though.

Wicket

Wicket (http://wicket.apache.org) is another MVC framework that now has native Guice support. Since version 1.3.0, the framework comes with a plug-in for Guice 1.0 that allows you to use Guice throughout your Wicket application. Unfortunately, the framework hasn't been designed with DI from the ground up like Struts 2; you only get the injectMembers(...) level of control for your Wicket WebPage implementations or other web artifacts. That's not horrible, but it does mean that you don't get to use constructor injection, scopes, and AOP in the web layer.

However, unlike the Struts plug-in, the Wicket plug-in handles the Injector's Stage correctly. When you set your Wicket application's configuration type to "deployment", Stage.PRODUCTION will be used. By default, or by setting the configuration type to "development", Stage.DEVELOPMENT will be used. For more information on configuring you application's configuration type, see the Wicket FAQ at http://cwiki.apache.org/WICKET/faqs.html.

Caution: At the time of this writing, Wicket is at 1.3.0-rc2, which still has a nasty bug described here: http://cwiki.apache.org/WICKET/guice-integration-pitfall.html. Basically, if you do bind not to an interface but to a concrete class, your concrete class *must* have a no-argument constructor. This bug is so ugly that I can't possibly recommend the Wicket Guice plug-in until it's fixed.

Here's what you need to do to set up Wicket with Guice.

1. Download the Wicket 1.3.0 distribution from http://wicket.apache.org.
2. Drop the wicket-guice jar along with all the dependencies in the WEB-INF/lib directory of your web application. See Table 5-1 for a complete listing of the library's dependencies. A list of dependencies can also be found in the README file that comes with the distribution.

3. Configure a `WicketFilter` in your `web.xml` file (`http://cwiki.apache.org/WICKET/migrate-13.html`). There, you need to set your root Guice `Module`, as I describe next.

Table 5-1. Example WEB-INF/lib Contents for Using Wicket with Guice

FRAMEWORK	JAR FILES	COMMENT

Guice	`guice-1.0.jar`
	`aopalliance.jar`
	`guice-servlet-1.0.jar`
		Only `guice-1.0.jar` is necessary if you don't use AOP or web scopes. The examples in this chapter will use only core Guice, but I'm including the other ones anyway.

Wicket	`wicket-1.3.0.jar`
	`slf4j-api-1.4.3.jar`
	`slf4j-jdk14-1.4.3.jar`
	`wicket-ioc-1.3.0.jar`
	`asm-1.5.3.jar`
	`cglib-nodep-2.1_3.jar`
	`wicket-guice-1.3.0.jar`
		You can choose any Simple Logging Facade for Java (SLF4J) implementation (`http://www.slf4j.org`).

Jetty	`jetty-6.1.6.jar`
	`jetty-util-6.1.6.jar`
	`servlet-api-2.5-6.1.6.jar`
		`servlet-api-2.5.6.1.6.jar` is entirely optional, but you do need `servlet-api` to compile, and I use Jetty as the web container (`http://www.mortbay.org`).

To set up the Guice configuration for your Wicket application, there are currently three options, two of which involve configuring the `WicketFilter` and I'll discuss these first. The easiest way to go is probably to configure a single root `Module` to use for the application. This can be seen in the Listing 5-5.

Listing 5-5. Wicket web.xml File that Configures a Guice Root Module

```
<?xml version="1.0" encoding="UTF-8"?>
<!DOCTYPE web-app
    PUBLIC "-//Sun Microsystems, Inc.//DTD Web Application 2.3//EN"
    "http://java.sun.com/dtd/web-app_2_3.dtd">
<web-app>
```

```xml
    <display-name>Wicket Guice</display-name>
    <filter>
        <filter-name>WicketFilter</filter-name>
        <filter-class>
            org.apache.wicket.protocol.http.WicketFilter
        </filter-class>
        <init-param>
            <param-name>applicationFactoryClassName</param-name>
            <param-value>
                org.apache.wicket.guice.GuiceWebApplicationFactory
            </param-value>
        </init-param>
        <init-param>
            <param-name>module</param-name>
            <param-value>
                hellowicket.WicketModule
            </param-value>
        </init-param>
        <init-param>
            <param-name>configuration</param-name>
            <!-- deployment or development -->
            <param-value>deployment</param-value>
        </init-param>
    </filter>
    <filter-mapping>
        <filter-name>WicketFilter</filter-name>
        <url-pattern>/*</url-pattern>
    </filter-mapping>
</web-app>
```

In this module, `hellowicket.WicketModule` in this example, you need to bind `WebApplication.class` to your application's implementation. Also don't forget to install any other modules that you were planning on using. Listing 5-6 shows an example that goes with the configuration in Listing 5-5.

Listing 5-6. The WicketModule Used in web.xml

```java
public class WicketModule extends AbstractModule {
    protected void configure() {
        // mandatory!
        bind(WebApplication.class).to(HelloGuiceApplication.class);
        // other bindings you want to use
        install(new HelloGuiceModule());
    }
}
```

The second option you have for configuring Wicket so that it uses Guice is to set Wicket to get the `Injector` from the `ServletContext` (to represent the applicationwide state). Coincidentally, this was exactly the strategy I used in the "Bootstrapping" section in this chapter, when I was talking about integrating with raw servlet-type applications. Later, in the "Dynamic Configuration" section, I extended the `GuiceServletContextListener` to be able to pick up a root `Module` from `web.xml`. It turns out that I can reuse that exact code with Wicket. So first, take a look at Listing 5-4 and then look at the `web.xml` file in Listing 5-7.

Listing 5-7. Configuring Wicket to Get the Injector from ServletContext

```
<?xml version="1.0" encoding="UTF-8"?>
<!DOCTYPE web-app
    PUBLIC "-//Sun Microsystems, Inc.//DTD Web Application 2.3//EN"
    "http://java.sun.com/dtd/web-app_2_3.dtd">

<web-app>
    <display-name>Wicket Guice</display-name>

    <!-- This one is needed in the GuiceServletContextListener -->
    <context-param>
        <param-name>module</param-name>
        <!-- has WebApplication.class bound -->
        <param-value>hellowicket.WicketModule</param-value>
        <description>Guice Module to load on startup</description>
    </context-param>

    <filter>
        <filter-name>WicketFilter</filter-name>
        <filter-class>
            org.apache.wicket.protocol.http.WicketFilter
        </filter-class>
        <init-param>
            <param-name>applicationFactoryClassName</param-name>
            <param-value>
                org.apache.wicket.guice.GuiceWebApplicationFactory
            </param-value>
        </init-param>
        <init-param>
            <param-name>injectorContextAttribute</param-name>
            <!-- The name of the ServletContext attribute
                used in GuiceServletContextListener -->
            <param-value>com.google.inject.Injector</param-value>
```

```
        </init-param>
        <init-param>
            <param-name>configuration</param-name>
            <!-- deployment or development -->
            <param-value>deployment</param-value>
        </init-param>
    </filter>
    <filter-mapping>
        <filter-name>WicketFilter</filter-name>
        <url-pattern>/*</url-pattern>
    </filter-mapping>

    <listener>
        <listener-class>
            discovery.GuiceServletContextListener
        </listener-class>
    </listener>
</web-app>
```

The Wicket plug-in will look at the attribute in the ServletContext, which has the name you specify as an <init-param> to the WicketFilter. In my GuiceServletContextListener found in Listing 5-4, the key is chosen as follows:

```
public static final String KEY = Injector.class.getName();
```

At runtime, KEY has the value of com.google.inject.Injector, which is, therefore, the value I needed to specify at injectorContextAttribute <init-param> for the WicketFilter. Here's what happens when the application starts:

1. The web container (Jetty in my case) will fire the contextInitialized event on the GuiceServletContextListener.

2. GuiceServletContextListener will get the module <context-param> and create the Injector with an instance of the Module with the Class name that was specified.

3. GuiceServletContextListener stores the Injector in the ServletContext with key com.google.inject.Injector.

4. WicketFilter is initialized, looks up the value for its injectorContextAttribute <init-param> (com.google.inject.Injector), and gets the Injector from the ServletContext using that value as the key

This is an example of the flexibility that you have when you are able to create the Injector yourself. Often, creating the Injector yourself might not make that much sense, but I was able to reuse code that I made earlier, when Wicket wasn't in the picture at all. Know that it's possible, but also know that the first approach is a lot simpler if you don't need the extra flexibility.

The third option is to hard-code Guice support into your WebApplication derivate, by registering an instance of the GuiceComponentInjector class (see Listing 5-8).

Listing 5-8. Hard-Coding Guice Support with Wicket

```
public class HelloGuiceApplication extends WebApplication {
    @Override
    protected void init() {
        addComponentInstantiationListener(
            new GuiceComponentInjector(this, new HelloGuiceModule()));
    }

    @Override
    public Class<?> getHomePage() {
        return Welcome.class;
    }
}
```

Using this option, your WicketFilter configuration is a lot simpler, but you've also hard-coded a dependency on Guice. You also don't register the WebApplication class in a Module now; you configure it directly in the web.xml file, as shown in Listing 5-9.

Listing 5-9. Simplest WicketFilter Configuration

```
<?xml version="1.0" encoding="UTF-8"?>
<!DOCTYPE web-app
    PUBLIC "-//Sun Microsystems, Inc.//DTD Web Application 2.3//EN"
    "http://java.sun.com/dtd/web-app_2_3.dtd">

<web-app>
    <display-name>Wicket Example</display-name>
    <filter>
        <filter-name>WicketFilter</filter-name>
        <filter-class>org.apache.wicket.protocol.http.WicketFilter</filter-class>
        <init-param>
          <param-name>applicationClassName</param-name>
          <param-value>hellowicket.HelloGuiceApplication</param-value>
```

```
        </init-param>
    </filter>
    <filter-mapping>
        <filter-name>WicketFilter</filter-name>
        <url-pattern>/*</url-pattern>
    </filter-mapping>
</web-app>
```

If you want to see the fully working example, take a look at the Hello Wicket Guice example in the appendix of this book. Alternatively, there's also a small Wicket-Guice example on the Wicket project web site.

GUICE SUPPORT FOR YOUR FAVORITE FRAMEWORK

This book mainly discusses Wicket and Struts 2 as web frameworks, because those frameworks' Guice plug-ins are part of an official effort *and* have the most traction in the community. You might be disappointed if your favorite web framework isn't one of those, but seriously, don't let that bring you down. First, creating a plug-in for a web framework is not as hard as you would think. For example, there are many more frameworks that currently support the Spring Framework. In many ways, integrating Guice will be similar, so there's no reason you couldn't learn from those existing plug-ins and implement support for it.

That said, there are some other *unofficial* efforts for web frameworks that I'm not going to talk much about. I have a couple of links handy, so I might as well share them with you; maybe you will find them useful. I have to say that I didn't try out all of these integration efforts, but if you Google your favorite framework, something might show up.

JSF: http://notdennisbyrne.blogspot.com/2007/10/integrating-guice-and-jsf-part-2.html

Stripes: http://article.gmane.org/gmane.comp.java.stripes.user/3418

GWT: http://radialmind.blogspot.com/2007/03/guice-in-gwt.html

Where Are the Web Scopes?

All this web integration stuff raises interesting questions: How do you integrate the Guice web scopes with all this framework code? More importantly, when you configure all these filters in the web.xml file, which one goes first? This is important, because web requests go through the filters in the order that they appear in web.xml. To make sure that the Guice scopes work as expected, register the GuiceFilter before any other framework filter. Listing 5-10 provides an example, taken directly from Guice's Struts 2 example.

Listing 5-10. Using the Guice Scope Filter in Conjunction with the Struts 2 Filter

```
<?xml version="1.0"?>
<!DOCTYPE web-app PUBLIC "-//Sun Microsystems, Inc.//DTD Web Application 2.3//EN"
  "http://java.sun.com/dtd/web-app_2_3.dtd">

<web-app>

  <filter>
    <filter-name>guice</filter-name>
    <filter-class>com.google.inject.servlet.GuiceFilter</filter-class>
  </filter>

  <filter>
    <filter-name>struts2</filter-name>
    <filter-class>org.apache.struts2.dispatcher.FilterDispatcher</filter-class>
  </filter>

  <filter-mapping>
    <filter-name>guice</filter-name>
    <url-pattern>/*</url-pattern>
  </filter-mapping>

  <filter-mapping>
    <filter-name>struts2</filter-name>
    <url-pattern>/*</url-pattern>
  </filter-mapping>

</web-app>
```

Warp Servlet

There's a whole ecosystem of open source Guice extensions over at `http://www.wideplay.com`:

- *Warp Persist*: Hibernate and JPA integration (including annotation-driven transactions)

- *Dynamic Finders*: Extension to Warp Persist for DAO-less persistence

- *Warp MVC*: A RESTful, component-based, event-driven web framework

- *Warp Servlet*: Advanced Guice web integration

Note: Most of the extensions at `http://www.wideplay.com` were written by Dhanji R. Prasanna, technical reviewer for this book—smart guy, smart code.

I will discuss and use the first two extensions from the preceding list in the next chapter. The Warp MVC framework is a bit early in its development to dedicate a section to it, but make sure to take a look at it because it looks very promising.

Warp Servlet is a project that takes Guice Servlet API integration to the next level. The solutions to the challenge I described at the beginning of this chapter look half-baked compared to the ones that can be found in this project. Unlike Warp MVC, Warp Servlet is not an MVC framework; it is a drop-in replacement for Guice's current and future Guice servlet integration and currently includes the following features:

- Guice-managed servlets and filters

- Mapping servlets and filters to URIs using regular expressions

- Request, session, and *flash* scope, that is, two consecutive requests' (see `http://www.theserverside.com/patterns/thread.tss?thread_id=20936` for more information)

Users of JBoss' Seam framework (http://www.jboss.com/products/seam) will be happy to hear that the project will include a conversation Scope in the near future. This is a scope that keeps state for an arbitrary number of requests and is often used for implementing wizard-type functionality. People historically tend to use the session scope for this type of workflow but often forget to clean up when the user operation finishes. Nobody likes memory leaks, so handing off this kind of risk to this conversation scope sounds like a solid plan.

I know what you were probably thinking just now, "This guy just told me that Guice can't create HttpServlet or Filter objects because the web container does, and now he's telling me that there's a project that does exactly that?" Well, I admit that this sounds confusing. The simplest possible explanation for this is that Warp Servlet only *appears* to be using "real" servlets and filters. In a classic web application, HTTP requests arrive, pass through the configured filters that match on the URI, and eventually end up at the Servlet match for that URI. Conceptually, this could look like Figure 5-1.

Figure 5-1. Classic servlet architecture

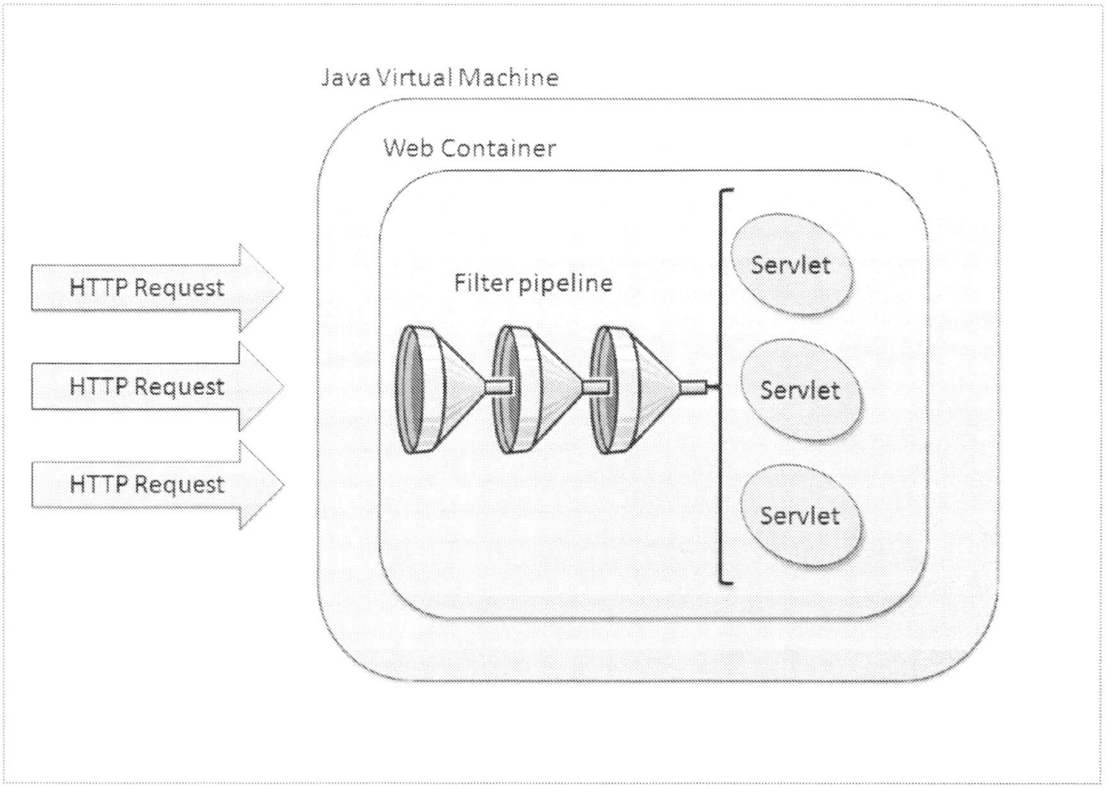

With Warp Servlet, you configure a `Filter` class that gets to handle all requests first. Using that filter, Warp Servlet is able to bypass the classic web container functionality and maintain its own `Filter` pipeline and set of servlets, using the same Servlet API classes. With some imagination, that configuration could look something like Figure 5-2.

Figure 5-2. How Warp Servlet's WebFilter changes the architecture

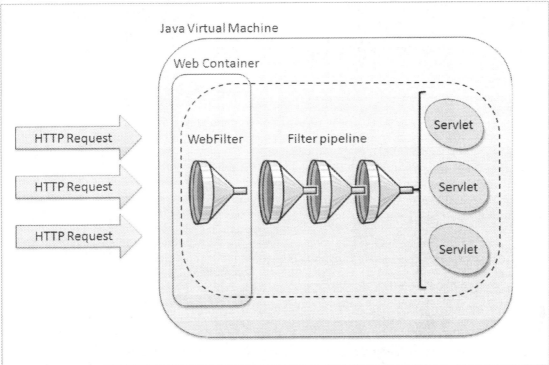

For Warp Servlet to be able to manage these Filter and Servlet instances, it needs you to configure them using Warp Servlet's API. That means that you don't put entries in the web.xml file like you're used to; instead, you use a builder-style API that feels natural to Guice. Fortunately, Warp Servlet makes sure that Servlet or Filter life cycle events like init(...) and destroy(...) get called just as the container would. You won't notice the difference between the Warp Servlet ones and the real deal.

What you *do* put in web.xml are the WebFilter and your subclass of WarpServletContextListener that creates your Injector. Let's take a look at an example in Listing 5-11.

Listing 5-11. An Example Warp Servlet web.xml

```xml
<?xml version="1.0" encoding="UTF-8"?>
<!DOCTYPE web-app
    PUBLIC "-//Sun Microsystems, Inc.//DTD Web Application 2.3//EN"
    "http://java.sun.com/dtd/web-app_2_3.dtd">

<web-app>
    <display-name>Hello Warp Servlet</display-name>
    <filter>
        <filter-name>WebFilter</filter-name>
        <filter-class>com.wideplay.warp.servlet.WebFilter</filter-class>
    </filter>
    <filter-mapping>
        <filter-name>WebFilter</filter-name>
        <url-pattern>/*</url-pattern>
    </filter-mapping>
    <listener>
        <listener-class>
            warpservlet.HelloGuiceServletContextListener
        </listener-class>
    </listener>
</web-app>
```

The `HelloGuiceServletContextListener` class in this example is my
`WarpServletContextListener` subclass. Notice that I didn't configure any servlets
(or filters) at this point. If you want Warp Servlet to manage them, you need to
configure them in the listener, like in Listing 5-12.

Listing 5-12. WarpServletContextListener Subclass

```java
package warpservlet;

import helloguice.HelloGuiceModule;

import com.google.inject.Guice;
import com.google.inject.Injector;
import com.wideplay.warp.servlet.Servlets;
import com.wideplay.warp.servlet.WarpServletContextListener;
```

```java
public class HelloGuiceServletContextListener extends WarpServletContextListener {
    @Override
    protected Injector getInjector() {
        return Guice.createInjector(
                new HelloGuiceModule(), // application bindings
                Servlets.configure()
                        .filters()
                        .servlets().serve("/*").with(HelloServlet.class)
                        .buildModule());
    }
}
```

Unlike in the "Inviting Servlets to the Club" section, you no longer need to override your Servlet's init(...) method, as shown in Listing 5-13.

Listing 5-13. Guice Just Works for HelloServlet

```java
public class HelloServlet extends HttpServlet {
    private final String appName;

    @Inject
    public HelloServlet(@Named("app.name") String appName) {
        // app.name configured in the HelloGuiceModule
        this.appName = appName;
    }

    @Override
    public void doGet(HttpServletRequest req, HttpServletResponse resp)
                throws ServletException, IOException {
        resp.setContentType("text/html");
        PrintWriter writer = resp.getWriter();
        writer.printf("<h1>Welcome to the %s application!</h1>%n", appName);
        resp.setStatus(HttpServletResponse.SC_OK);
    }
}
```

More information on Warp Servlet or one of the other Warp projects can be found on the Wideplay web site (http://www.wideplay.com). And remember, Warp Servlet offers a superset of the functionality Guice Servlet offers. Don't use both.

Summary

Guice 1.0 does not ship with any raw web integration code. Although it's not that hard to roll your own servlet integration, you're better off using an MVC framework, like Struts 2 or Wicket 1.3.0, that can support Guice natively through a plug-in. I had to be honest in this chapter; some of the plug-ins don't offer the quality you've come to expect from high-profile open source projects. But Struts 2 especially is a natural fit for DI and the plug-in's minor issues can easily be fixed, so let's hope that Bob and the Guice team release an update soon.

An alternative to the raw guice-servlet support is Warp Servlet. It offers the best possible Guice integration for raw servlets and filters and supports some Guice scopes out of the box, like request, session, and flash. This simplifies the configuration that needs to happen on your side. Warp Servlet is definitely worth considering in addition to an MVC framework's Guice integration or when you're not using an MVC framework at all.

Chapter 6: Practical Guice

Like any other cool new technology, Guice will be a viable solution only if it helps you solve real-life problems, like connecting to a database or interacting with the user through a web interface. By now, you can probably imagine how that would work in the Guice world, so let's take a look at how all the pieces fit together.

Requirements

In this chapter, we're going to discuss the *Shopping List* sample application. The goal of the application is to be able to manage daily or weekly shopping lists. The user thinks of something to buy on shopping day (like coffee or an iPod) and logs on to the application to add the item to one of the shopping lists. Here's the short list of requirements:

- The user can log on to the secured area of the application.

- On the welcome screen, the user sees a summary of shopping lists.

- The user can create a shopping list containing one or more products and give it a name.

- The user can view the contents of a shopping list.

- The user can update an existing shopping list.

- An existing shopping list can be deleted from the system.

Because the point of this chapter is to learn from an application that resembles something you would build in real life, and because this is a book on Guice, I'd also like to add the following nonfunctional requirements.

- The application has to be Guice powered.

- The application has to use a database and an ORM framework. I'm going with Hibernate, through the Java Persistence API (JPA).

- The application has to use an MVC web framework. I'm going with Struts 2.

On the other hand, the application will completely ignore some parts that are not important to the discussion:

- Allowed users will be hard-coded.

- Authentication will be lightweight (but fully functional).

- The product list will be fixed.

- No caching strategy will be used.

- The application will not use any templating technology like Tiles (http://tiles.apache.org).

- We'll assume the graphical designer got fired early in the process (my eyes!).

I think it is also important to know that I will focus on very specific areas of the application for this chapter. This will not be a tutorial in which you can just copy everything verbatim and expect the code to work. I will use the application I implemented for you as a starting point for discussing how you can integrate with Guice. Here is what I will discuss to help you get started:

- An overview of the application's Struts 2 architecture

- A quick look into the project structure of the application I built

After that, things really get interesting. I will focus on the following specific technical elements:

- Setting up Struts 2 and Guice

- Developing a domain model

- Setting up database access

- Coding the data access layer

- Getting the Struts actions to work with the data

Other functionality, like basic security, will be implemented in the eventual application but will not be discussed in detail. To try out the fully working application, including security and the like, I suggest that you download the source code from the Apress web site (http://www.apres.com). Feel free to contact me if you have any problems understanding the code.

Tip: To learn about Struts 2, I recommend that you read a book like *Struts 2 In Action Struts 2 In Action* by Don Brown, Chad Davis, and Scott Stanlick (Manning, 2008).

The Big Picture

In Figure 6-1, you can see the Struts 2 architecture I came up with for this application. As you'll notice, there are three action classes:

- ShoppingListsAction *(top left)*: This is the gateway to the home screen, and it handles that screen's operations. This action is also the entry point for the application after authentication.

- ShoppingListAction *(bottom left)*: This handles the creation or updating of individual shopping lists.

- ProductListAction *(middle right)*: This is a special action; it gets called by the createSL and editSL views to get a list of available products, instead of being in the driver's seat itself.

Keep this figure in mind as you read the rest of this chapter; whenever you feel lost, revisit it.

Figure 6-1. A conceptual overview of the Shopping List application

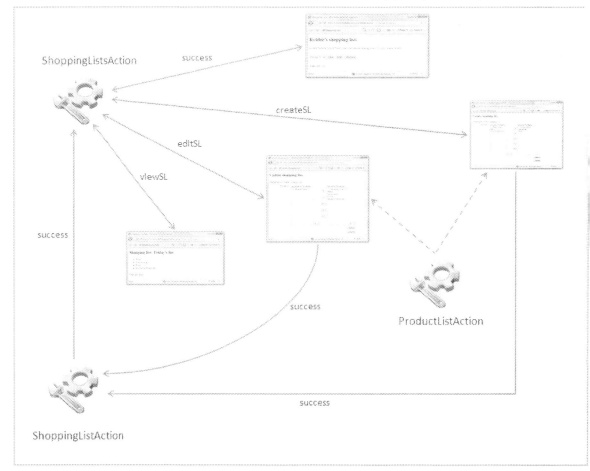

These action classes alone don't do much without actual view pages, so let me guide you through the application's screens in a visual fashion, using screenshots. This will help you understand all the code later on in the chapter.

First, there is the all-important home screen that displays the logged-in user's current shopping lists, as depicted in Figure 6-2.

Figure 6-2. The home screen

If you click the View button next to the "Friday's list" shopping list, you'll see something like Figure 6-3.

Figure 6-3 Viewing a shopping list screen

Next to the View button in Figure 6-2, there was also an Edit button. Clicking that one will result in Figure 6-4. As you can see, all available products have already been selected. The Remove button, the third one next to "Friday's list", simply removes the shopping list and returns to the home screen.

Figure 6-4. The screen to edit a shopping list

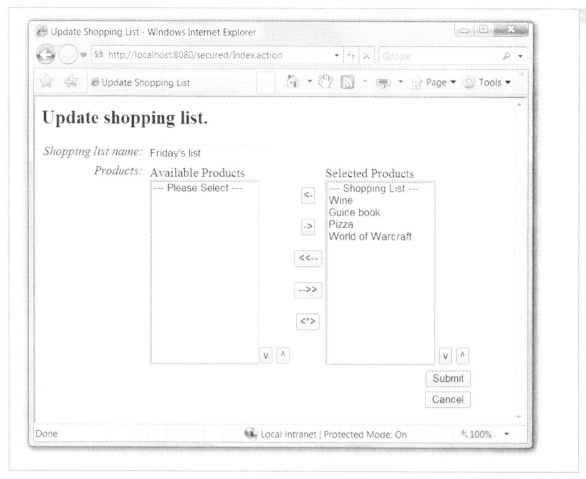

There's also the create screen shown in Figure 6-5, which is practically identical to the edit screen. To create a new shopping list using this page, you would use the Create text link shown in Figure 6-2.

Figure 6-5. The shopping list creation screen

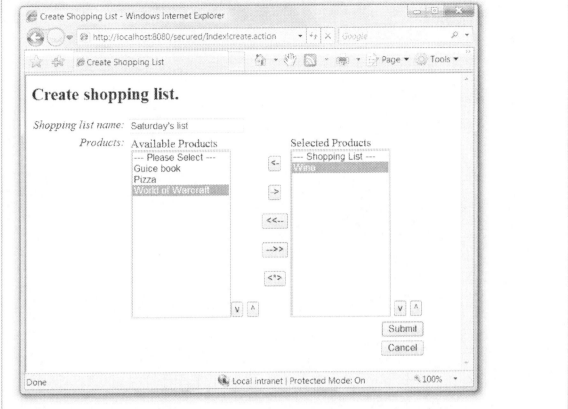

Now that you have a feel for what the Shopping List application is about, let's take a look at how I set up the project structure and at which files go where.

Project Structure

Figure 6-6 shows how my Eclipse project setup looks for the Shopping List application. Don't worry about what everything means at this point, but I will use this figure as a reference later on in the chapter. To run the application, I use a simple class to start Jetty on the project structure that resembles an exploded WAR file. To make that work, I set my Eclipse compilation output directory to /WEB-INF/classes (which is also why it doesn't show up in the figure).

Figure 6-6. The Shopping List project's exploded WAR structure

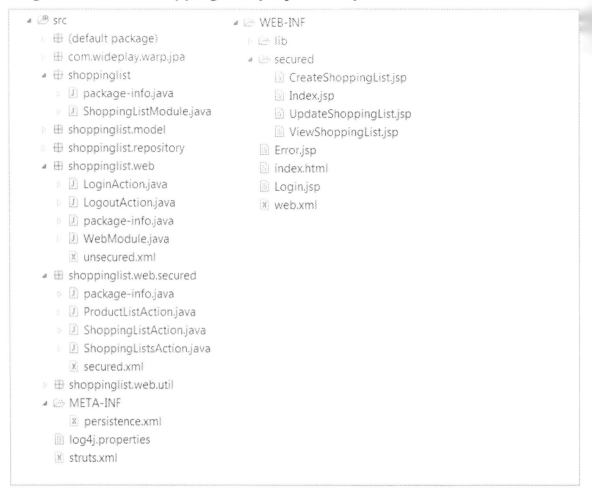

The most important things to note here are the action classes, shown in the shoppinglist.web.secured package, the various configuration files like the Struts configuration files (struts.xml, unsecured.xml, secured.xml), the persistence configuration (persistence.xml) and the obvious presence of a web.xml file.

Now, before I get into that, let's take a look at the JAR dependencies. Table 6-1 gives an overview of the JAR files I'm putting in WEB-INF/lib and where you can download them. This will be useful when you start developing your own applications and want to know what you need to get up and running.

Table 6-1. Shopping List Dependencies

PROJECTS AND LOCATIONS	DESCRIPTION	FILES TO INCLUDE
Jetty 6.1.6 http://www.mortbay.org	Web container	jasper-compiler-5.5.15.jar, jasper-compiler-jdt-5.5.15.jar, jasper-runtime-5.5.15.jar, ant-1.6.5.jar, commons-collections-2.1.1.jar, commons-el-1.0.jar, xmlParserAPIs-2.6.2.jar, jetty-6.1.6.jar, jetty-util-6.1.6.jar, jsp-api-2.0.jar, servlet-api-2.5-6.1.6.jar, and xercesImpl-2.6.2.jar
Guice 1.0 http://code.google.com/p/google-guice/	Guice (seriously ...)	guice-1.0.jar, guice-servlet-1.0.jar, guice-struts2-plugin-1.0.1.jar, and aopalliance.jar
Hibernate Core 3.2.5 Hibernate Annotations 3.3.0 Hibernate EntityManager 3.3.1 http://www.hibernate.org	ORM framework	hibernate3.jar, hibernate-annotations.jar, hibernate-commons-annotations.jar, hibernate-entitymanager.jar, hibernate-validator.jar, asm-attrs.jar, asm.jar, cglib-2.1.3.jar, javassist.jar, jboss-archive-browsing.jar, dom4j-1.6.1.jar, ejb3-persistence.jar, jta.jar, commons-logging-1.0.4.jar (also for Struts 2), and antlr-2.7.6.jar, log4j-1.2.11.jar (optional)

Table 6-1. Shopping List Dependencies (continued)

PROJECTS AND LOCATIONS	DESCRIPTION	FILES TO INCLUDE
Struts 2.0.11 http://struts.apache.org	MVC framework	`xwork-2.0.4.jar`, `struts2-core-2.0.11.jar`, `ognl-2.6.11.jar`, `commons-logging-1.0.4.jar`, and `freemarker-2.3.8.jar`
MySQL Connector/J 5.0.8 http://www.mysql.org	Database driver	`mysql-connector-java-5.0.8-bin.jar`
Warp Persist 1.0 http://www.wideplay.com	Persistence for Guice	`warp-persist-1.0.jar`

Besides the sheer volume of dependencies, I would like to call out two things from Table 6-1. First, Struts 2 has a hard dependency on `guice-servlet`, like I mentioned in the previous chapter. Second, I also added Warp Persist. I also talked briefly about Warp Persist in the previous chapter, so you probably already know that it's about providing Hibernate and JPA support to Guice. I'm going to use Warp Persist to interact with the database.

Talking about the database, you probably noticed that I included the MySQL driver. I'm going to use MySQL as the database for the sample application. I also installed MySQL GUI Tools, which allows you to manage your MySQL instance with a nice-looking UI. Both can be downloaded from the MySQL web site at `http://www.mysql.org`. Using the GUI tools, I created the sample application's database schema: `shopping_list`. I'm not going to bother with database security or table creation; that, I'll leave up to Hibernate.

Now, let's get going with the first item on the list: setting up Struts 2.

Setting Up Struts 2

The first step is to configure Struts's FilterDispatcher in the web.xml file. As the name suggests, this class will filter all incoming web requests and dispatch them as it sees fit. This is the class that makes Struts tick. Second, I need to configure the Guice web scopes, for reasons I already mentioned previously. Listing 6-1 shows web.xml, correctly configured to use both. Remember, the order matters.

Listing 6-1 Shopping List's web.xml

```xml
<?xml version="1.0" encoding="UTF-8"?>
<web-app id="WebApp"
         version="2.4"
         xmlns="http://java.sun.com/xml/ns/j2ee"
         xmlns:xsi="http://www.w3.org/2001/XMLSchema-instance"
         xsi:schemaLocation="http://java.sun.com/xml/ns/j2ee ➥
http://java.sun.com/xml/ns/j2ee/web-app_2_4.xsd">

    <display-name>Shopping List</display-name>

    <filter>
        <filter-name>guice</filter-name>
        <filter-class>com.google.inject.servlet.GuiceFilter</filter-class>
    </filter>

    <filter>
        <filter-name>struts2</filter-name>
        <filter-class>org.apache.struts2.dispatcher.FilterDispatcher</filter-class>
    </filter>

    <filter-mapping>
        <filter-name>guice</filter-name>
        <url-pattern>/*</url-pattern>
    </filter-mapping>

    <filter-mapping>
        <filter-name>struts2</filter-name>
        <url-pattern>/*</url-pattern>
    </filter-mapping>
    ...
</web-app>
```

I'm not going to overwhelm you with tons of Struts 2 configuration, so let's go right to the part that matters: setting up Guice. By the way, to see where all the files I talk about end up, keep one eye on Figure 6-6.

Tip: Buy two copies of this book to keep one eye on Figure 6-6. Just kidding!

Getting Guiced

To configure Guice, all I need to do is visit the struts.xml file and add two lines of configuration. Listing 6-2 highlights the needed additions.

Listing 6-2. Guice-Enabled struts.xml

```
<!DOCTYPE struts PUBLIC
    "-//Apache Software Foundation//DTD Struts Configuration 2.0//EN"
    "http://struts.apache.org/dtds/struts-2.0.dtd">
<struts>
    <constant name="struts.objectFactory" value="guice" />
    <constant name="guice.module" value="shoppinglist.ShoppingListModule" />
    ...
</struts>
```

Notice that I chose shoppinglist.ShoppingListModule as the root module. I've been using AbstractModule throughout the book, so I'll implement the Module interface directly for a change. Listing 6-3 shows the empty ShoppingListModule.

Listing 6-3. Empty ShoppingListModule

```
public class ShoppingListModule implements Module {
    public void configure(Binder binder) {
        // Do not need ServletModule
        // because the Struts plugin 1.0.1 installs it.
    }
}
```

That's all for the Guice side of things. That's also the last piece of Struts configuration you'll see in this chapter, so throw those hands up! When the party settles, move on to the next section, in which I will explain the domain model for the application.

Defining the Model

Before I can use and persist the Shopping List application's data using JPA and Hibernate, I first need to develop a model. Luckily, the Shopping List model is pretty simple. Looking back at the "Requirements" section, you can see that the primary artifacts to deal with here are shopping lists and the products that go on those shopping lists. I'm immediately going to map these artifacts to the shoppinglist and product database tables respectively, using the shopping_list schema I already created in my MySQL database (see the "Project Structure" section). Listing 6-4 shows my Product class, mapped to the product table using JPA annotations.

Listing 6-4. Product

```
package shoppinglist.model;
… // imports

@Entity
public class Product {
    private Long id;
    private String name;

    @GeneratedValue @Id
    public Long getId() {
        return id;
    }

    // other getters/setters
    // equals, hashCode, toString
}
```

Note that I don't need to provide a mapping for the name property; if there's a column in the database with the same name, Hibernate, my JPA implementation of choice, will figure out how to convert that value from and to the database. In fact, it does that for all non-transient fields.

The second model class is ShoppingList. Similar to Product, it will also have id and name properties. What's different here is that it's also linked to a given user's login name (e.g., Robbie), and it obviously contains a list of products. To get this relationship in the database, I'm going to map that list of products to a link table using both the shopping list ID and the product ID. This is a many-to-many relationship, but I'm only going to provide a mapping on the ShoppingList side. Listing 6-5 shows the ShoppingList class.

Listing 6-5. ShoppingList

```
package shoppinglist.model;
… // imports

@Entity
public class ShoppingList {
    private Long id;
    private String name;
    private String login;

    private List<Product> products;

    @GeneratedValue @Id
    public Long getId() {
        return id;
    }

    @ManyToMany(targetEntity=Product.class,
                cascade={CascadeType.PERSIST, CascadeType.MERGE})
    @JoinTable(name="shoppinglist_product",
                joinColumns={@JoinColumn(name="shoppinglist_id")},
                inverseJoinColumns={@JoinColumn(name="product_id")})
    public List<Product> getProducts() {
        return products;
    }

    // other getters/setters
    // equals, hashCode, toString
}
```

These mappings alone don't do much, so I still need to configure JPA to use Hibernate, and set the correct properties so that Hibernate can connect to the database. To do so, I created a META-INF directory in my source folder and added the JPA persistence.xml file shown in Listing 6-6. Putting that file in a META-INF directory in the classpath is a JPA requirement. You can see in Figure 6-6 where this file goes in the global picture.

106   Google Guice: Agile Lightweight Dependency Injection Framework

Listing 6-6. /src/META-INF/persistence.xml

```xml
<?xml version="1.0" encoding="UTF-8" ?>
<persistence xmlns="http://java.sun.com/xml/ns/persistence"
    xmlns:xsi="http://www.w3.org/2001/XMLSchema-instance"
    xsi:schemaLocation="http://java.sun.com/xml/ns/persistence
    http://java.sun.com/xml/ns/persistence/persistence_1_0.xsd"
    version="1.0">

    <!-- Local transactions. -->
    <persistence-unit name="shoppinglistJpaUnit"
        transaction-type="RESOURCE_LOCAL">
        <provider>org.hibernate.ejb.HibernatePersistence</provider>
        <class>shoppinglist.model.ShoppingList</class>
        <class>shoppinglist.model.Product</class>
        <properties>
            <property name="hibernate.show_sql" value="true" />
            <property name="hibernate.format_sql" value="true" />
            <property name="hibernate.connection.driver_class"
                    value="com.mysql.jdbc.Driver" />
            <property name="hibernate.connection.url"
                    value="jdbc:mysql://localhost/shopping_list" />
            <property name="hibernate.connection.username" value="root" />
            <property name="hibernate.connection.password" value="root" />
            <property name="hibernate.dialect"
                    value="org.hibernate.dialect.MySQL5Dialect" />
            <property name="hibernate.connection.autocommit" value="false"/>
            <!-- Let Hibernate create and manage the tables. -->
            <property name="hibernate.hbm2ddl.auto" value="update" />
        </properties>
    </persistence-unit>
</persistence>
```

The persistence.xml file shown in Listing 6-6 looks pretty standard, but let me point out two things here:

- I'm going to use local transactions.

- I'm going to let Hibernate create the database tables. It will generate the Data Definition Language (DDL) statements using the mapped ShoppingList and Product classes.

Now, JPA by itself is a great idea (partly because it looks so much like Hibernate), but sometimes, it requires you to do a lot of *manual* labor. For example, you'll often need to do things like this:

1. Start the persistence service.
2. Create an `EntityManagerFactory` instance.
3. Get an `EntityManager` instance.
4. Open up a transaction.
5. Do some work.
6. Commit or roll back the transaction.
7. Close the `EntityManager` instance.
8. Shut down the `EntityManagerFactory` instance.

In Enterprise JavaBeans (EJB) 3, of which JPA is a part, limited DI concepts were introduced that can help you with all this work. For example, you can have a fresh `EntityManager` instance injected whenever a method gets called on a session bean. Unfortunately, this injection is only possible inside an EJB 3 container and doesn't allow you to access lazily loaded collection properties on your entities outside of a session bean. There are ways to work around that, using patterns like Open Session In View, but that level of integration is not specified by the JPA.

Note: To learn about Open Session In View, take a look at `http://www.hibernate.org/43.html`. It's also worth mentioning that both Spring and JBoss Seam solve these problems in their own ways; the JBoss Seam documentation especially is an entertaining read: `http://docs.jboss.com/seam/latest/reference/en/html/persistence.html`.

As you can probably already guess, ease of use for JPA and providing DI functionality are areas where Guice could really shine. That's what Dhanji R. Prasanna must have thought when he created the Warp Persist project—a project that offers Guice integration for JPA and Hibernate and includes declarative transaction management through its use of Guice AOP.

Database Access with Warp Persist

As you can read at the Wideplay web site (http://www.wideplay.com), setting up Warp Persist is easy. Usually, you follow these steps:

1. Decide what you want to use: JPA with Hibernate, JPA with Toplink, Hibernate, and so on.
2. Choose a deployment strategy (e.g., session-per-transaction or session-per-request).
3. Create the needed framework configuration files (e.g., persistence.xml).
4. Annotate your methods with @Transactional where appropriate.
5. Build a Warp Persist module (e.g., specify a unit of work based on the deployment strategy) and include it when creating the injector.

For web applications, it's nearly always best to go for the session-per-request strategy, which is similar to the Open Session In View pattern I mentioned earlier.

If you try to set things up as described on the Wideplay web site, you'll notice that you run into errors pretty quickly when you try to use their SessionPerRequestFilter class. This has nothing to do with the quality of their documentation but is a problem specific to Struts 2 and the Guice plug-in. For Struts to be able to make use of SessionPerRequestFilter, you need to configure it to go *before* the Struts FilterDispatcher entry in the web.xml file. This ensures that a JPA EntityManager instance or Hibernate Session instance is available when a request hits Struts. Unfortunately, there are no guarantees that Guice has been started at that point because of how the current Guice plug-in is designed. Warp Persist's SessionPerRequestFilter needs information from Guice, but Guice hasn't been started yet when the first request arrives.

Unless the Guice folks change the design of the Struts 2 plug-in, you'll need a solution specific to Struts. Fortunately, Struts 2 already had a built-in concept similar to servlet filters: interceptors. This is stuff you shouldn't have to think about, so feel free to use the interceptor I built for you in this book's Appendix section titled "SessionPerRequestInterceptor."

Once you have the `SessionPerRequestInterceptor` configured as described in the Appendix, you need to add the Guice configuration to configure Warp Persist. Listing 6-7 shows the module that I will include at `Injector` creation.

Listing 6-7. RepositoryModule

```
package shoppinglist.repository;
… // imports
public class RepositoryModule extends AbstractModule {
    @Override
    protected void configure() {
        // Warp Persist
        // "shoppingListJpaUnit" matches the name in the persistence.xml
        bindConstant().annotatedWith(JpaUnit.class).to("shoppinglistJpaUnit");
        install(PersistenceService.usingJpa()
                        // EntityManager spans HTTP Request
                        .across(UnitOfWork.REQUEST)
                        .transactedWith(TransactionStrategy.LOCAL)
                        .buildModule());
    }
}
```

To start using this `RepositoryModule`, I install it in the `ShoppingListModule`, which is the module I configured in the `struts.xml` to create the `Injector` with. Listing 6-8 shows my modified `ShoppingListModule`.

Listing 6-8. Persistence-Enabled ShoppingListModule

```
public class ShoppingListModule implements Module {
    public void configure(Binder binder) {
        // Do not need ServletModule
        // because the Struts plugin 1.0.1 installs it.

        binder.install(new RepositoryModule());
    }
}
```

Installing `RepositoryModule` concludes the steps you need to take to get JPA and Hibernate up and running. Now, let's take a look at how I'm going to *use* JPA and Hibernate, by implementing the data access layer.

Implementing the Data Access Layer

The first thing I'm going to implement is the ShoppingListRepository class, which as the name suggests, will provide the necessary CRUD operations for use with the ShoppingList model class. In Listing 6-9, you can see the interface I came up with.

Listing 6-9. ShoppingListRepository

```
package shoppinglist.repository;
// imports…
public interface ShoppingListRepository {
    void create(ShoppingList shoppingList);
    void update(ShoppingList shoppingList);
    void delete(ShoppingList shoppingList);
    List<ShoppingList> findShoppingLists(String login);
}
```

Now, I need to create an implementation of this interface that talks to the database. And when you start doing data access, you need to start thinking about transactions. Luckily, Warp Persist supports declarative transaction management, so all I need to do to make the repository methods transactional is annotate them with the @Transactional annotation.

To get hold of a JPA EntityManager instance that will handle all the database work, I can simply inject an instance that Warp Persist automatically configures. You need to be careful though; inject Provider<EntityManager> or scope ShoppingListRepository to match the Warp Persist UnitOfWork configured earlier in RepositoryModule. This makes sure you don't perform a scope-widening injection, which is what would happen if you would inject the EntityManager directly into a singleton.

Take a look at my ShoppingListRepository implementation, called JpaShoppingListRepository, in Listing 6-10.

Note: Scope widening will be discussed in the next chapter.

Listing 6-10. JpaShoppingListRepository

```java
package shoppinglist.repository;

import java.util.List;

import javax.persistence.EntityManager;

import shoppinglist.model.ShoppingList;

import com.google.inject.Inject;
import com.google.inject.Provider;
import com.google.inject.name.Named;
import com.wideplay.warp.persist.Transactional;

public class JpaShoppingListRepository implements ShoppingListRepository {
    // Use a Provider, or scope this class to match the WP UnitOfWork
    private final Provider<EntityManager> em;

    @Inject
    public JpaShoppingListRepository(Provider<EntityManager> em) {
        this.em = em;
    }

    @SuppressWarnings("unchecked")
    @Transactional
    public List<ShoppingList> findShoppingLists(String login) {
        return (List<ShoppingList>)em.get()
                .createQuery("SELECT sl FROM ShoppingList sl " +
                             "WHERE sl.login = :login ORDER BY sl.name ASC")
                .setParameter("login", login)
                .getResultList();
    }

    @Transactional
    public void create(ShoppingList shoppingList) {
        em.get().persist(shoppingList);
    }

    @Transactional
    public void update(ShoppingList shoppingList) {
        em.get().merge(shoppingList);
    }
```

```
@Transactional
public void delete(ShoppingList shoppingList) {
    em.get().remove(shoppingList);
}
}
```

You can see that using Warp Persist makes the whole thing look rather simple. The only method that looks a little bit ugly is findShoppingLists(...), with @SuppressWarnings and all.

Besides the fact that I should use a named query instead of hard coding the query code, there's another improvement possible. Warp Persist has a feature called *dynamic finders*, which enables you to get rid of all the boilerplate code for queries. In fact, you can get rid of *all* the code besides the actual query. Here's how:

```
@Finder(query="SELECT sl FROM ShoppingList sl " +
                   "WHERE sl.login = :login ORDER BY sl.name ASC")
@Transactional
public List<ShoppingList> findShoppingLists(@Named("login") String login) {
    return null;
}
```

This findShoppingLists(...) method now returns null, or at least, so it seems. Using Guice AOP, Warp Persist will intercept this method, and it will generate an implementation for you. Warp Persist never even calls the actual method, so you could return whatever you want; the code will never execute.

Now, let's put a named query on ShoppingList. That way, Hibernate can validate that query at startup, and I can more easily reuse it. Listing 6-11 highlights the changes needed to the ShoppingList class.

Tip: Usually, you should put @Transactional not on data access methods directly but on service classes or even controllers. Because this application doesn't have a service layer and doesn't need more coarse-grained transactions, I'm simply configuring my repositories to be transactional.

Listing 6-11. Named Query Added to ShoppingList

```
@Entity
@NamedQuery(name=ShoppingList.Q_SHOPPING_LIST_FOR_LOGIN,
            query="SELECT sl FROM ShoppingList sl " +
                  "WHERE sl.login = :login ORDER BY sl.name ASC")
public class ShoppingList {
    public static final String Q_SHOPPING_LIST_FOR_LOGIN = "shoppingListsForLogin";

    … // fields, getters, setters, …
}
```

Now, I can change the findShoppingLists(...) method to use the named query:

```
@Finder(namedQuery=ShoppingList.Q_SHOPPING_LIST_FOR_LOGIN)
@Transactional
public List<ShoppingList> findShoppingLists(@Named("login") String login) {
    return null;
}
```

WARP PERSIST ANNOTATION SEMANTICS

You can also apply @Finder to methods on interfaces or abstract classes—but keep in mind that @Transactional doesn't work on those finders, because Warp Persist does its own proxying for interfaces and abstract methods to make dynamic finders work. This means that Guice AOP, which powers @Transactional, will not work on those finders. To use @Transactional in such a case, you'll need to apply transactions in a logical software layer above the data access layer, which is probably a good idea anyway.

Another interesting fact about Warp Persist is that you can limit the number of classes that Warp Persist proxies. You do this by manipulating its Guice AOP configuration. Here's an example:

```
install(PersistenceService.usingJpa()
        .across(UnitOfWork.REQUEST)
        .transactedWith(TransactionStrategy.LOCAL)
        // Transactions for any class, methods annotated with CustomAnnotation
        .forAll(any(), annotatedWith(CustomAnnotation.class))
        .buildModule());
```

One final thing you need to do is add a binding for JpaShoppingListRepository, as shown in Listing 6-12. I'm binding it in the singleton scope, because it makes sense to reuse the same instance over and over again.

Listing 6-12. ShoppingListRepository Binding

```java
public class RepositoryModule extends AbstractModule {
    @Override
    protected void configure() {
        // Warp Persist
        // "shoppingListJpaUnit" matches the name in the persistence.xml
        bindConstant().annotatedWith(JpaUnit.class).to("shoppinglistJpaUnit");
        install(PersistenceService.usingJpa()
                            // EntityManager spans HTTP Request
                            .across(UnitOfWork.REQUEST)
                            .transactedWith(TransactionStrategy.LOCAL)
                            .buildModule());

        bind(ShoppingListRepository.class)
            .to(JpaShoppingListRepository.class)
            .in(Singleton.class);
    }
}
```

This is it for the ShoppingListRepository implementation. Now, I need to create something similar for the Product model class.

Tip: The code I just wrote for JpaShoppingListRepository is often nearly exactly the same for other model objects. Therefore, to get rid of this layer altogether and using the Generic DAO pattern often makes sense, as described in http://www-128.ibm.com/developerworks/java/library/j-genericdao.html and http://hibernate.org/328.html. That's right; the days of the DAO are numbered.

Not surprisingly, the repository for Product is called ProductRepository. Take a peek at the interface in Listing 6-13.

Listing 6-13. ProductRepository Interface

```
package shoppinglist.repository;

import java.util.List;

import shoppinglist.model.Product;

public interface ProductRepository {
    List<Product> getProducts();
    List<Product> getProductsById(List<Long> ids);
    List<Product> getProductsComplementOf(List<Product> products);
}
```

The implementation, again, will be done using Warp Persist. This time there are no write operations, so I'm going to use @Finder methods for all the queries. I could have put them on the interface directly, but then I wouldn't be able to put @Transactional on them (or doing so wouldn't help, at least). Listing 6-14 shows the implementation, JpaProductRepository.

Note: Since the most recent version of Warp Persist, 1.0, you can also put @Transactional at the class level to serve as a metaconfiguration for that class. But you can achieve the same results if you configure its Guice AOP settings as described earlier in the sidebar.

Listing 6-14. JpaProductRepository

```
public class JpaProductRepository implements ProductRepository {
    @Finder(namedQuery=Product.Q_ALL_PRODUCTS)
    @Transactional
    public List<Product> getProducts() {
        return null;
    }

    @Finder(namedQuery=Product.Q_PRODUCTS_WITH_IDS)
    @Transactional
    public List<Product> getProductsById(@Named("ids") List<Long> ids) {
        return null;
    }
```

```
@Finder(namedQuery=Product.Q_PRODUCTS_COMPLEMENT)
    @Transactional
    public List<Product> getProductsComplementOf(
                         @Named("products") List<Product> products) {
        return null;
    }
}
```

Like JpaShoppingListRepository, JpaProductRepository uses named queries, so I need to define those in the Product class! Listing 6-15 shows their definitions.

Listing 6-15. Named Queries Added to Product

```
@Entity
@NamedQueries({
    @NamedQuery(name=Product.Q_PRODUCTS_COMPLEMENT,
                query="SELECT p FROM Product p WHERE p NOT IN(:products)"),
    @NamedQuery(name=Product.Q_PRODUCTS_WITH_IDS,
                query="SELECT p FROM Product p WHERE p.id IN(:ids)"),
    @NamedQuery(name=Product.Q_ALL_PRODUCTS, query="SELECT p FROM Product p")
})
public class Product {
    public static final String Q_PRODUCTS_COMPLEMENT = "productsComplement";
    public static final String Q_PRODUCTS_WITH_IDS = "productsWithIds";
    public static final String Q_ALL_PRODUCTS = "allProducts";

    ... // fields, getters, setters, ...
}
```

Then, only the Guice configuration is left, so I add a binding to RepositoryModule as shown in listing 6-16.

Listing 6-16. RepositoryModule with JpaProductRepository Configured

```
public class RepositoryModule extends AbstractModule {
    @Override
    protected void configure() {
        // The other bindings
        ...

        bind(ProductRepository.class)
            .to(JpaProductRepository.class)
            .in(Singleton.class);
    }
}
```

That is all: I've now implemented the data access layer. I added some repository implementations using Warp Persist, added bindings to the RepositoryModule, and installed that module in the ShoppingListModule, which is the module Guice will use, as configured in the struts.xml. Next, let's take a look at all three actions shown in Figure 6-1 starting with the ShoppingListsAction that drives the home screen.

The Home Screen

After logging in, the user should get to see a list of all her shopping lists. Also, from that page, it should be possible to view, edit, or remove a shopping list or to create a new one. This navigation from and to the home screen is what the ShoppingListsAction will handle. In case you can't remember, this is the action at the top left in Figure 6-1.

Without going into every detail: The home screen view iterates over a collection of ShoppingList items for the current user; this is a value that ShoppingListsAction will need to provide. Listing 6-17 shows the action.

Listing 6-17. ShoppingListsAction

```
/**
 * Actions related to collections of {@link ShoppingList} instances.
 */
public class ShoppingListsAction extends ActionSupport {
    // Data sources
    private final ShoppingListRepository shoppingListRepo;
```

```java
private final Provider<UserToken> userToken;

// UI
private Map<String, String> view = newHashMap();
private Map<String, String> edit = newHashMap();
private Map<String, String> remove = newHashMap();

// State
private List<ShoppingList> shoppingLists;
private ShoppingList shoppingList;

@Inject
public ShoppingListsAction(ShoppingListRepository shoppingListRepo,
                           Provider<UserToken> userToken) {
    this.shoppingListRepo = shoppingListRepo;
    this.userToken = userToken;
}

//-----------------------------------------------------------------------
// Action methods
//-----------------------------------------------------------------------

public String execute() {
    this.shoppingLists = shoppingListRepo.
                            findShoppingLists(userToken.get().getLogin());
    if (view.size() > 0) return view();
    if (edit.size() > 0) return edit();
    if (remove.size() > 0) return remove();
    return SUCCESS;
}

private String view() {
    shoppingList = currentShoppingList(view);
    return "viewSL";
}

private String edit() {
    shoppingList = currentShoppingList(edit);
    return "editSL";
}

private String remove() {
    // delete the source data
    shoppingListRepo.delete(currentShoppingList(remove));
    // update the in-memory list
    shoppingLists.remove(currentShoppingListIndex(remove));
```

```
        return SUCCESS;
    }

    public String create() {
        return "createSL";
    }

    // other Struts 2 code
}
```

You probably noticed that the constructor gets injected by Guice, through my use of the Guice @Inject annotation. The constructor takes two parameters: one ShoppingListingRepository and a Provider<Usertoken> instance, which is a Guice Provider that returns an instance of the UserToken class. I already configured ShoppingListRepository, so let's take a look at what this UserToken is about.

The UserToken class identifies a user session. When a user successfully logs in, I put a UserToken instance in the session containing the user's login name. This UserToken instance goes in HttpSession, which is equivalent to the session scope in Guice. Now, to shorten the work I need to do in actions, I created Provider<UserToken> to remove a layer of indirection for me. Instead of manipulating the session directly, the Provider<UserToken> instance does the manipulation, and as a result, my action code is much cleaner. So, take a look at my WebModule shown in Listing 6-18, which I'll also install in ShoppingListModule. WebModule is the module that contains all web related dependencies.

Tip: You could use a similar provider mechanism for transcending scopes. But that's not what I need here.

Listing 6-18. Removing Indirection with a Provider

```
package shoppinglist.web;
… // imports

public class WebModule extends AbstractModule {
    @Override
    protected void configure() {
        bind(UserToken.class).toProvider(new Provider<UserToken>() {
            @Inject private HttpSession session;
```

```
        public UserToken get() {
            // Struts 2 synchronizes on the same object
            synchronized (session) {
                return (UserToken) session.getAttribute(UserToken.KEY);
            }
        }
    }); // no scope!
    }
}

package shoppinglist;
… // imports
public class ShoppingListModule implements Module {
    public void configure(Binder binder) {
        // Do not need ServletModule
        // because the Struts plugin 1.0.1 installs it.

        binder.install(new RepositoryModule());
        binder.install(new WebModule());
    }
}
```

One action down, two to go—on to the create and edit screens!

The Create and Edit Screens

If you look closely at Figure 6-1, you'll see that both the editSL and the createSL view pages call ProductListAction to get a list of available products. In the JSPs, this looks something like the following:

```
<%-- Call another action to get the productList --%>
<s:action name="ProductList" id="productList">
    <%-- Don't load all products for selection when editing --%>
    <s:param name="selectedProducts" value="shoppingList.products"/>
</s:action>
```

The preceding code gets either all of the products stored in the database or, in the case of an edit, all of the products but the ones that are already selected. Listing 6-19 shows the ProductListAction action that handles those requests.

Listing 6-19. ProductListAction

```
public class ProductListAction {
    private final ProductRepository productRepo;
    private List<Product> productList;
    private List<Product> selectedProducts;

    @Inject
    public ProductListAction(ProductRepository productRepo) {
        this.productRepo = productRepo;
    }

    public String execute() {
        if (this.selectedProducts == null)
            this.productList = productRepo.getProducts();
        else
            this.productList = productRepo
                            .getProductsComplementOf(this.selectedProducts);
        return Action.SUCCESS;
    }

    public List<Product> getProductList() {
        return productList;
    }

    public void setSelectedProducts(List<Product> selectedProducts) {
        this.selectedProducts = selectedProducts;
    }
}
```

Notice the dependency on ProductRepository, which I already configured. Besides that, this action has no dependencies, so I'm all done here. I'll have more of that, please.

Listing 6-20 shows the ShoppingListAction, which is the action that processes shopping list submissions from the createSL or editSL views. Again, this class uses the repositories created earlier, so no real work here. My prayers have been answered!

Listing 6-20. ShoppingListAction

```java
/**
 * Actions related to a single {@link ShoppingList}.
 */
public class ShoppingListAction extends ActionSupport {
    private ShoppingList shoppingList;
    private Long[] selectedProducts;

    private final ShoppingListRepository shoppingListRepository;
    private final ProductRepository productRepo;

    @Inject
    public ShoppingListAction(ShoppingListRepository repository,
                              ProductRepository productRepo) {
        this.shoppingListRepository = repository;
        this.productRepo = productRepo;
    }

    //-------------------------------------------------------------------
    // Data manipulation
    //-------------------------------------------------------------------

    public String createSubmit() {
        shoppingList.setProducts(
            productRepo.getProductsById(Arrays.asList(getSelectedProducts())));
        shoppingListRepository.create(shoppingList);
        return SUCCESS;
    }

    public String editSubmit() {
        shoppingList.setProducts(
            productRepo.getProductsById(Arrays.asList(getSelectedProducts())));
        shoppingListRepository.update(shoppingList);
        return SUCCESS;
    }

    // getters, setters …
}
```

Unit Testing

Now, how should you go about unit testing this Guice application? Simple: you don't need to use Guice. Because of your DI-style (inversion of control) design, you can easily create mock dependencies to test classes in isolation. Listing 6-21 shows an example test for `ProductListAction`. In real life, you will also want to consider the use of a mocking framework like EasyMock (`http://www.easymock.org`).

Tip: There's a testing framework with Guice support out there. Check out AtUnit (`http://code.google.com/p/atunit/`).

Listing 6-21. ProductListActionTest

```java
public class ProductListActionTest {
    @Test
    public void returnsAllProducts() {
        ProductRepository mockRepo = new ProductRepository() {
            public List<Product> getProducts() {
                return productList();
            }
            public List<Product> getProductsById(List<Long> ids) {
                return null; // never used
            }
            public List<Product> getProductsComplementOf(List<Product> products) {
                return null; // never used
            }
        };
        ProductListAction pa = new ProductListAction(mockRepo);
        pa.execute();
        assertEquals(productList(), pa.getProductList());
    }

    private List<Product> productList() {
        Product p1 = newProduct(1L, "name1");
        Product p2 = newProduct(2L, "name2");
        return Arrays.asList(p1, p2);
    }

    private Product newProduct(Long id, String name) {
        Product p = new Product(); p.setId(id); p.setName(name);
        return p;
    }
}
```

Note: I'm a fan of test-driven development, but I deliberately did not take that road for this chapter to keep the content easily digestible.

Summary

In this chapter, I tried to give you a better idea of what it takes to build a Guice-powered application. I think the most important thing to take away here is that it is *dead simple*. Other than that, I think I also delivered proof of the following:

- Warp Persist makes data access a breeze.

- Using modules will make your application layers more visible.

- You can use providers to remove levels of indirection.

- You don't need Guice when you write unit tests.

You can download the full source code to the Shopping List application from the Apress web site at http://www.apress.com.

Chapter 7: Guice Recipes

When you learn any new framework or programming language, picking up the basics usually doesn't take you very long. People tend to learn by reference—once you know how a for loop works in C, understanding similar concepts in other programming languages becomes incredibly easy. Similarly but more in the context of this book, if you already have experience with DI frameworks like the Spring Framework or PicoContainer, you probably didn't have much trouble understanding how Guice works.

Some knowledge, however, can only come from experience with the framework and by discussing ideas with the community. This chapter aims to give you a head start and discusses various best practices and commonly asked questions I've collected over the past year or so, as well as some of Guice's smaller features like integration with the Spring Framework or JNDI.

Sharing Singletons

While a singleton is a fairly simple concept, there is one mistake that beginning Guice users often make. Take a look at Listing 7-1. What does it print?

Listing 7-1. Drinkable Carbonated Water

```
interface Drinkable {}
interface Carbonated {}
class Water implements Drinkable, Carbonated {}

public class SharingSingletons {
    public static void main(String[] args) {
        Injector i = Guice.createInjector(new AbstractModule() {
            protected void configure() {
                bind(Drinkable.class).to(Water.class).in(Singleton.class);
                bind(Carbonated.class).to(Water.class).in(Singleton.class);
            }
        });
        Drinkable drinkable = i.getInstance(Drinkable.class);
        Carbonated carbonated = i.getInstance(Carbonated.class);
        System.out.println(drinkable == carbonated);
    }
}
```

When you run this example, you'll see that it prints false. Looking at the configuration, however, this might seem strange at first.

For the most part, I think confusion sets in because Guice comes with a scope that's named "singleton" that doesn't produce *real* singletons in the classic design pattern sense. Think about it: when you ask Guice for a singleton, what do you really want?

- One instance per JVM and per type?
- One instance per Injector and per type?
- One instance per Injector and per Key (i.e., per binding)?

If you go back to Guice's singleton scope description in Chapter 2,"Enter Guice," you'll realize that Guice's singleton scope implements the third option: you'll get one instance per Injector and per Key.

That said, the reason why Listing 7-1 prints false is twofold:

- Scopes always work per Key; bindings to different type and binding annotation combinations will always spawn different instances no matter what the scope.
- The element specified in the to(...) method actually *refers to another binding*. The ability to bind to a Class instance directly is merely a convenience: Guice *always* binds to a Key internally. This means that a scope never applies to the to(...) element of a binding; it already has a scope of its own.

Caution: Bindings to different keys will always spawn different instances no matter what the scope, *unless* the scope implementation at hand purposely discards some of that information, for example, the annotation. Currently, this is not the case for any existing Guice scope; they all use Key to identify bindings just like Guice itself does.

In this example case, there is no explicit binding for Water, but as you know, Guice always has an implicit binding (in "no scope") ready for concrete classes.

Both of the bindings shown in Listing 7-1 receive a distinct "no scope" Water instance. To make the example in Listing 7-1 return true, you simply replace Guice's implicit binding to Water with your own explicit binding that binds Water in the singleton scope. Both the bindings in the previous listing can then bind to your explicit Water binding and thus receive that singleton instance. After that, because the target Water instance already is a singleton, the Drinkable and Carbonated bindings also no longer need to have the singleton scope applied. Listing 7-2 shows the configuration that returns true.

Listing 7-2. A Manual Per-Injector and Per-Type Instance

```
bind(Water.class).in(Singleton.class);
bind(Drinkable.class).to(Water.class);
bind(Carbonated.class).to(Water.class);
```

If you now wanted to have one type instance per JVM, I suggest that you roll your own Scope implementation. Try to stay away from manual singletons: they are error prone and make testing your code harder.

Binding Collections

A question that often comes up is, "How can I bind a set of objects in a collection?" Guice's Binding EDSL makes it easy to bind isolated objects, but it's also easy to get lost when you want to start binding collections of objects, like lists or maps. How should one approach this issue? Well, as you've probably heard your local consultant say, it depends. I think you can split this problem up into three types of collection content:

- Objects that are not managed by Guice (or don't need to be)

- Objects that are managed by Guice

- Objects that will exist in the future and make use of a future Guice version

Let's take a look at these one at a time. For the first type of content, let's revisit the fortune cookie example from Chapter 1. Listing 7-3 shows the FortuneService that gives out random fortunes.

Listing 7-3. Not Very Guicy FortuneServiceImpl

```
public interface FortuneService { String randomFortune(); }

public class FortuneServiceImpl implements FortuneService {
    private static final List<String> MESSAGES =
        Arrays.asList(
            "Today you will have some refreshing juice.",
            "Larry just bought your company."
        );

    public String randomFortune() {
        return MESSAGES.get(new Random().nextInt(MESSAGES.size()));
    }
}
```

As you can see, the list of fortunes currently gets created in a static variable. Using Guice, you can do better. Listing 7-4 displays a Guicier approach.

Listing 7-4. Guicy FortuneServiceImpl

```
public class FortuneServiceImpl implements FortuneService {
    private final List<String> messages;

    @Inject
    public FortuneServiceImpl(List<String> messages) {
        this.messages = messages;
    }

    public String randomFortune() {
        return messages.get(new Random().nextInt(messages.size()));
    }
}
```

Because the fortunes in the list are just strings, they don't need to be managed by Guice. For a list containing only unmanaged objects, which is what the first type of collection content is all about, you should consider using a provider. Listing 7-5 shows an example.

Listing 7-5. A Fortune Provider

```
public class FortuneListProvider implements Provider<List<String>> {
    public List<String> get() {
        return Arrays.asList(
            "Today you will have some refreshing juice.",
            "Larry just bought your company."
        );
    }
}
```

Note: You could use toInstance(...) to achieve the same result as Listing 7-5, but I advise against it. Although it's not horrible to make use of it in this case (this example looks like a constant binding), you should develop the habit of not using it. Otherwise, chances are that you'll start using it to bootstrap more expensive services that have a higher risk of failing, like database connections. Starting up Guice should be fast and predictable—move the risk to your code.

Using this provider, you can now bind the fortune list. Listing 7-6 shows you how the pieces fit together.

Listing 7-6. Collection Binding for Unmanaged Objects

```
public class Main {
    public static void main(String[] args) {
        Injector i = Guice.createInjector(new AbstractModule() {
            protected void configure() {
                bind(new TypeLiteral<List<String>>(){})
                    .toProvider(new FortuneListProvider())
                    .in(Singleton.class);

                bind(FortuneService.class).to(FortuneServiceImpl.class);
            }
        });
        FortuneService fortuneService = i.getInstance(FortuneService.class);
        System.out.println(fortuneService.randomFortune());
    }
}
```

As you would expect, the example shown in Listing 7-6 prints a random fortune on the console: Larry just bought your company.

The second type of collection contents are managed objects, objects that *are* in the club. Let's go back to the same fortunes example. Recall MegaFortuneService from Chapter 2? If not, use Listing 7-7 to refresh your memory.

Listing 7-7. MegaFortuneService

```
public class MegaFortuneService implements FortuneService {
    private static final List<FortuneService> SERVICES =
        Arrays.<FortuneService>asList(
            new FunnyFortuneService(),
            new QuoteFortuneService()
        );

    public String randomFortune() {
        ...
    }
}
```

Just like the FortuneServiceImpl in Listing 7-3, this class also holds a list of objects in a static variable. Again, let's convert this class to a "don't call us, we'll call you" design, as shown in Listing 7-8.

Listing 7-8. Guicy MegaFortuneService

```
public class MegaFortuneService implements FortuneService {
    private final List<FortuneService> services;

    @Inject
    public MegaFortuneService(List<FortuneService> services) {
        this.services = services;
    }

    public String randomFortune() {
        ...
    }
}
```

This time, the list contains not dumb String objects but fortune services. It's not too hard to imagine that these services themselves want to have dependencies injected. If so, such a collection of managed objects changes the binding game.

First, take a look at Listing 7-9 to see how the module configuration looks *before* I bind the collection.

Listing 7-9. All MegaFortuneService Dependency Bindings Without List<FortuneService>

```
public class MegaModule extends AbstractModule {
    protected void configure() {
        bind(FortuneService.class)
            .annotatedWith(Funny.class)
            .to(FunnyFortuneService.class);

        bind(FortuneService.class)
            .annotatedWith(Quote.class)
            .to(QuoteFortuneService.class);

        // MegaFortuneService that contains a list of the other two.
        bind(FortuneService.class)
            .annotatedWith(Mega.class)
            .to(MegaFortuneService.class);
    }
}
```

The most obvious option now would be to bind List<FortuneService> to a Provider instance. Listing 7-10 illustrates this approach.

Listing 7-10. FortuneServiceListProvider

```
public class FortuneServiceListProvider implements Provider<List<FortuneService>> {
    @Inject @Quote FortuneService quoteService;
    @Inject @Funny FortuneService funnyService;
    public List<FortuneService> get() {
        return Arrays.asList(quoteService, funnyService);
    }
}

public class MegaModule extends AbstractModule {
    protected void configure() {
        … // the other bindings

        bind(new TypeLiteral<List<FortuneService>>(){})
            .toProvider(new FortuneServiceListProvider())
            .in(Singleton.class);
    }
}
```

The drawback of this provider approach is that you have to inject all the possible fortune services into the FortuneServiceListProvider manually. This can be a major pain if your lists are very large or have varying elements depending on the modules you use. For example, if the FunnyFortuneService and QuoteFortuneService bindings would reside in two different modules, you always need to include them both at Injector-creation time, unless you start using @Inject(optional=true) in the provider and start checking for null references when you create the actual list. This explosion of configuration code is what you should try to avoid.

To do so, I suggest that you consider using a more object-oriented approach. To achieve the maximum amount of flexibility, you could let the services add themselves to the list, instead of adding them to the list manually in a provider. Listing 7-11 shows this approach; note that you need to bind the services as eager singletons to make sure that they've registered themselves at application start-up.

Listing 7-11. A Registry/Visitor Style of Design

```
public class FunnyFortuneService implements FortuneService {
    @Inject
    public void register(List<FortuneService> services) {
        services.add(this);
    }
    ...
}

public class QuoteFortuneService implements FortuneService {
    @Inject
    public void register(List<FortuneService> services) {
        services.add(this);
    }
    ...
}

public class MegaModule extends AbstractModule {
```

```
protected void configure() {
    //bind(FortuneService.class)
    //    .annotatedWith(Funny.class)
    //    .to(FunnyFortuneService.class);
    //bind(FortuneService.class)
    //    .annotatedWith(Quote.class)
    //    .to(QuoteFortuneService.class);

    // Binding services is simpler now, but you need asEagerSingleton()
    bind(FunnyFortuneService.class).asEagerSingleton();
    bind(QuoteFortuneService.class).asEagerSingleton();

    // MegaFortuneService that contains a list of the other two.
    bind(FortuneService.class)
        .annotatedWith(Mega.class)
        .to(MegaFortuneService.class);

    // No longer bind to Provider
    //bind(new TypeLiteral<List<FortuneService>>(){})
    //    .toProvider(new FortuneServiceListProvider())
    //    .in(Singleton.class);

    // Bind the List<FortuneService> to an empty ArrayList
    bind(new TypeLiteral<List<FortuneService>>(){})
        .to(new TypeLiteral<ArrayList<FortuneService>>(){})
        .in(Singleton.class);
    }
}
```

Note: You don't really *need* to bind the collection elements as eager singletons when using the approach in Listing 7-11. For example, you could set up the dependencies in such a way that the collection elements would always come up first.

As you can see in Listing 7-11, this approach requires you to factor collection bindings into your application's design. This is not horrible, but I think this is a problem Guice could (and probably will) address. That's why I included the third category about future Guice implementations. To track the current progress on this issue, which the Guice folks call multibindings, take a look at issue number

37 in the Guice issue tracker: `http://code.google.com/p/google-guice/issues/detail?id=37`.

Tip: Guice currently does not feature life cycle event support, but you could use this last design to achieve something like it. For example, you could collect all classes that implement a `ShutdownListener` interface and iterate over the resulting collection in `GuiceServletContextListener`.

Designing Libraries and Limiting Visibility

You've undoubtedly heard of the "limit visibility" mantra. Reducing the conceptual surface of an API has several advantages, including these:

- Users have less to learn.

- Getting into trouble is harder for users.

- You don't *have* to write as much JavaDoc documentation.

- The API will be easier to get right.

In Java, you get both the tools (private, protected, etc.) and the building blocks (classes, fields, etc.) to achieve this goal. With Guice in the picture, you get some new building blocks to put in your API: modules and binding annotations. It's important that you think about how this changes the API design game. When you do, you'll realize that there are two new practices at your disposal:

- *Hiding implementation classes*: By making your implementation classes package private (the default access) and having at least one public module per package, you can avoid leaking implementation details and prevent your users from tightly coupling with the API. This will help ensure that your users fall into the pit of success.

- *Hiding individual bindings*: By making certain binding annotations package private, you can prevent them from being used externally, even if they are defined in a publicly available module. Doing this makes sense only in combination with the first practice, though.

That said, a related question that often pops up in the Guice community is, "How can I go about designing libraries that use Guice?" For example, you might want to create a library that uses Guice internally and make that library available to other developers, so you'd need to

- Provide a solid API that has one well-defined programming model
- Bootstrap Guice

The first problem can be solved using the two new practices I just listed. The second one, however, seems to be a big hurdle for a lot of people.

In the ideal world, you *and* your users would be using Guice. In such a case, the solution is simple: you *don't* bootstrap Guice. You just provide the modules, using the practices I described earlier in this section, and let your users consume them. When they create their Injector instances, they can specify (or import, if you will), the modules that go with the packages they want to use. Alternatively, you could also provide one *root* module that installs all the other modules for the library at once.

Tip: In that ideal world in which both you and your users are using Guice, you will probably want to consider dynamically loading modules, depending on which JARs are in the classpath. See the "Configuration Discovery" section in Chapter 5 to learn about some of your options there.

Now, if your users *don't* use Guice, you're in trouble; you basically have three choices:

- Make them use Guice directly.
- Make them use Guice indirectly.
- Don't enforce the use of Guice.

I already discussed how you would approach the first option, so let's move right on to the second one. If your users can't (or don't want to) use Guice, you could consider creating some kind of façade class that they will have to use as a starting point for any work they want to do with your library. Under the hood, that class would then manage an Injector instance and give out Guice-managed objects. This scenario is kind of awkward and getting the scoping right will be tricky, but it can work if you set your mind to it. All in all, I don't recommend this option.

The third option is not to enforce the use of Guice. You could configure the library for use with Guice, for example, to annotate injection points, create binding annotations, and provide modules. Then, you could leave it up to your users to decide whether they want to use Guice or use your library with Spring or another DI framework. Shipping a Guice-enabled API is an interesting option but also limits what you can do in terms of modern design. For example, you won't be able to make all implementation classes package private.

Note: In my opinion, this section alone proves that Guice, or something like Guice, should be in Java SE. Imagine a world in which all libraries include the necessary annotations for DI use. The power! The simplicity!

Viral Annotations

Binding annotations are one of Guice's most innovative features. However, people new to Guice often seem to be a bit skeptical. For example, let's say you use @Fast Computer everywhere in your code. Then, at some point in the future, you would like to switch to the @VeryFast Computer. This poses an interesting challenge, because making the switch would require you to change your code all over the place. Do binding annotations spread like a virus?

Yes and no. I think this is a problem that, in essence, will always exist: if there are multiple implementations that you want to use next to each other, you will need to be specific. This is no different when using factories or other DI frameworks. Usually, you can work around the problem, though, and it turns out that using an all-Java framework like Guice helps a lot in some cases. Here are some tips to help you on your quest for maintainable code:

- Only be specific if you have to be. If there is only one implementation, don't use a binding annotation.

- Don't be too specific when choosing the annotation name. For example, `@Performant Computer` might describe the component well enough.

- Design your application with care. If you have the same dependency in half of the classes in your application, that's a sign you need to refactor. Usually, you can also confine certain dependencies to a logical layer; for example, you would only use a Hibernate `Session` in the data access layer.

- Use your IDE's refactoring tools. For example, if you're no longer going to use `@Fast`, just rename `@Fast` to `@VeryFast`, and let the IDE do all the work for you. This is when Guice is really the captain of the football team. With Guice on the team, all the other players (e.g., the IDE) play the game of their lives.

- Avoid using `@Named` as much as possible. String identifiers can be harder to refactor.

Mixing Scopes

You'll definitely agree with me that scopes are a very useful Guice feature. If you want an object to be request scoped, all you have to say is, "Tag! You're a request-scoped object!" Having this power available with so little effort is probably a good thing, but as the saying goes, with great power comes great responsibility.

When you mix and match two class instances in your application, there are three scoping options:

- The scope of class A is wider than the scope of class B.

- The scope of class A is equal to the scope of class B.

- The scope of class A is narrower than the scope of class B.

The caveat is in the first option. If you want an instance of class A to work properly until the application exits or until it is no longer needed, you need to make sure that all its dependencies (e.g., B) stay in place until the very end. If one of the dependencies fails to live as long as the instance itself, it's almost guaranteed that you will get into trouble. This is what is called a *scope widening injection*: by injecting a dependency of a narrower scope, you artificially *widen* its lifetime to match the lifetime of the target object (the one that's injected). Because class A holds references to all its dependencies, they can not be garbage collected until the class A instance itself dies. So it is very possible that the scope where the dependency objects live has died a long time ago, but the garbage collector simply doesn't get the chance to clean up the waste because the A instance still holds references to zombie objects.

Let me give you a realistic example (shown in Figure 7-1). Say you have a singleton A instance and an HTTP-request-scoped B instance. If A loads eagerly, you get lucky, and Guice will tell you right away (with OutOfScopeException) that there is a problem when it tries to inject B. When the HTTP request scope is not active, you will not be able to create your singleton object. However, Guice is not always able to help you out (at least not in version 1.0).

Let's say A does *not* load eagerly and instead loads when the first HTTP request comes in. In that case, the HTTP request scope *is* active, and A will be created successfully. All subsequent requests will then reuse the same A instance (since it's a singleton), and that A instance holds a reference to a B dependency that was in scope during the first request, and only the first request. This is obviously dangerous and might result incorrect program behavior, crashes, or you getting fired.

Figure 7-1. Scope widening: creating a singleton A instance with a request-scoped B instance dependency

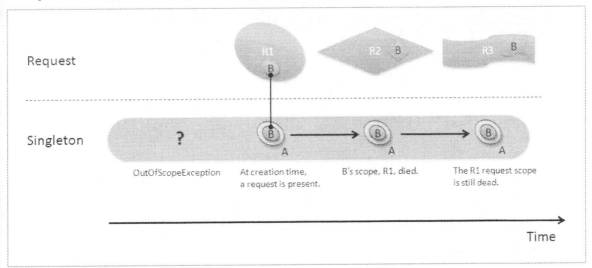

That said, there are two ways (that I know of) to approach this scope widening pitfall:

- Pay attention so that you do not to perform a scope widening injection anywhere in your application.

- Inject `Provider<B>` into A, and only access B when you are sure it is in currently in scope.

This is all the advice I can give you at this point. Perhaps, in a future version of Guice, there will be some way to specify interscope dependencies, so that you can say, "Singleton scope is wider than session scope, and session scope is wider than request scope." With that information, Guice could then throw an exception when an injection goes from right to left in the scope relationship (when it widens) instead of from left to right.

Integrating Spring

Through the `guice-spring-1.0.jar` file that comes with the Guice 1.0 distribution, Guice offers limited integration with the Spring Framework. More specifically, it enables you to bind existing Spring beans as Guice objects.

The plug-in supports the following two binding scenarios:

- You bind all the Spring beans from a given `BeanFactory` or `ApplicationContext` as Guice objects that match the following injection point: `@Named("beanName")` `BeanType`.

- You bind the Spring `BeanFactory` or `ApplicationContext` directly and have the ability to generate providers for your own bindings. These providers will look up the Spring beans that have the name and type you supply.

Caution: The Guice integration for Spring respects the Spring prototype and singleton scopes, but disregards other scopes. If your Spring beans use another scope, I advise against the use of this extension until support for other scopes (request, session, etc.) is added.

Let's take a look at a small example. Imagine you configure the class shown in Listing 7-12 using Spring.

Listing 7-12. MySpringBean

```
package chapter7.spring;

public class MySpringBean {
    private String message;

    public void sayHello() {
        System.out.print("Hello"+this.message);
    }

    public void setMessageUsingSpring(String message) {
        this.message = message;
    }
}
```

MySpringBean's configuration could look like the XML shown in Listing 7-13.

Listing 7-13. MySpringBean Spring Configuration

```xml
<?xml version="1.0" encoding="UTF-8"?>
<beans xmlns="http://www.springframework.org/schema/beans"
       xmlns:xsi="http://www.w3.org/2001/XMLSchema-instance"
       xsi:schemaLocation="http://www.springframework.org/schema/beans
           http://www.springframework.org/schema/beans/spring-beans-2.5.xsd">

    <bean id="mySpringBean" class="chapter7.spring.MySpringBean">
        <property name="messageUsingSpring" value=" world!"/>
    </bean>

</beans>
```

First, let's take a look at the simplest approach: letting Guice bind all available Spring beans (one in this case) to @Named("beanName") BeanType. For this example, that would be @Named("mySpringBean") MySpringBean. Listing 7-14 shows this approach.

Listing 7-14. Letting Guice Generate Bindings for All Spring Beans

```java
import static com.google.inject.spring.SpringIntegration.bindAll;

public class SpringToGuice {
    private static ClassPathXmlApplicationContext springContext() {
        ...
    }

    public static void main(String[] args) {
        Injector i = Guice.createInjector(new AbstractModule() {
            protected void configure() {
                bindAll(binder(), springContext());
            }
        });
        i.getInstance(NeedsSpringDependency.class);
    }
}

public class NeedsSpringDependency {
    @Inject
    NeedsSpringDependency(@Named("mySpringBean") MySpringBean springBean) {
        springBean.sayHello();
    }
}
```

This example prints "Hello world!" and proves that the Guice dependency injected in the NeedsSpringDependency class originally was a Spring bean, because I configured Spring to set the "world!" part of the output (see Listing 7-13) .

The second approach is to simply bind the BeanFactory type to your BeanFactory or ApplicationContext instance and let Guice generate individual providers for you, for a given type and Spring bean name. This allows you to choose the binding annotation yourself (if you choose to use one) instead of having to use the default @Named("mySpringBean"). Listing 7-15 demonstrates this approach, using the same example as the previous approach.

Listing 7-15. Binding Spring Beans Using Generated Providers

```java
import static com.google.inject.spring.SpringIntegration.fromSpring;
import static com.google.inject.name.Names.named;

public class SpringToGuice {
    private static ClassPathXmlApplicationContext springContext() {
        ...
    }

    public static void main(String[] args) {
        Injector i = Guice.createInjector(new AbstractModule() {
            protected void configure() {
                // I know, I know, toInstance...
                bind(BeanFactory.class).toInstance(springContext());

                bind(MySpringBean.class)
                    .annotatedWith(named("annotationOfMyChoice"))
                    .toProvider(fromSpring(MySpringBean.class, "mySpringBean"));
            }
        });
        i.getInstance(NeedsSpringDependency.class);
    }
}

public class NeedsSpringDependency {
    @Inject
    NeedsSpringDependency(@Named("annotationOfMyChoice") MySpringBean springBean) {
        springBean.sayHello();
    }
}
```

Like the previous example, this example also prints "Hello world!"

Logging

Guice logs some (performance-related) information to its JDK logger. If you are not accustomed to using the logging system that comes with the JDK, take a look at Listing 7-16. This listing shows a simple utility class that I made with which you can enable Guice logging output on the console.

Listing 7-16. GuiceDebug

```
public class GuiceDebug {
    private static final Handler HANDLER = new ConsoleHandler() {{
        setLevel(Level.ALL); setFormatter(new Formatter() {
            public String format(LogRecord r) {
                return String.format("[Guice] %s%n", r.getMessage());
            }
        });
    }};

    private GuiceDebug() {}

    public static void enable() {
        Logger guiceLogger = Logger.getLogger("com.google.inject");
        guiceLogger.addHandler(GuiceDebug.HANDLER);
        guiceLogger.setLevel(Level.ALL);
    }
}
```

If you execute GuiceDebug.enable() before you start Guice, you should see something like the following on the console:

```
[Guice] Configuration: 59ms
[Guice] Binding creation: 48ms
[Guice] Binding indexing: 0ms
[Guice] Validation: 0ms
[Guice] Static validation: 1ms
[Guice] Static member injection: 1ms
[Guice] Instance injection: 1ms
[Guice] Preloading: 1ms
```

Now, chances are that you are not using JDK logging in your application. To unify JDK logging with Log4J, Commons Logging, and whatnot, you can use SLF4J (http://www.slf4j.org). You will want to use their JDK logging handler, which can be found at `http://bugzilla.slf4j.org/attachment.cgi?id=15`; it allows you to route the Guice logs to your favorite logging system.

Integrating JNDI

As a testimony of the flexibility of providers, Guice 1.0 ships with very simple but effective JNDI integration. It allows you to get a value from JNDI without **all** the exception handling hassle and without the use of a service locator. Take a look at Listing 7-17.

Listing 7-17. Guice JNDI Integration

```
import javax.naming.Context;
import javax.naming.InitialContext;
import javax.sql.DataSource;

import com.google.inject.AbstractModule;
import static com.google.inject.jndi.JndiIntegration.*;

public class JndiModule extends AbstractModule {
    @Override
    protected void configure() {
        // Bind a Context, the default InitialContext for example.
        bind(Context.class).to(InitialContext.class);

        // fromJndi generates a Provider.
        bind(DataSource.class)
            .toProvider(fromJndi(DataSource.class, "java:comp/env/jdbc/MyDS"));
    }
}
```

First, you need to bind a JNDI `Context` object. Typically, using a default `InitialContext` instance is sufficient, so I'm going with that. Next, using the `JndiIntegration` class, you can generate a `Provider` instance for a given type and JNDI location. When that `Provider` instance is invoked when running the application, it will simply return the object at the specified JNDI location. It's that simple!

> **Tip:** Did you know that Eclipse's Content Assist (Ctrl+Space bar) feature can suggest static imports in the more recent versions? All you need to do is specify your commonly used classes in Window → Preferences → Java → Editor → Content Assist → Favorites.

Using JMX

Guice has built-in support to inspect an `Injector`'s bindings at runtime using the Java Management Extensions (JMX); see `http://java.sun.com/docs/books/tutorial/jmx/`). JMX is a technology that was added in Java SE 5, which Guice obviously requires, that enables you to inspect a running application and interact with objects called MBeans. These MBeans are nothing more than regular Java objects that follow a certain coding convention.

With little effort, Guice will create a series of MBeans for you from an `Injector`'s bindings. Guice will not expose all your Guice objects as MBeans; it exposes *only the objects' binding information*. It's not exceptionally hard to add a Guice-managed object as an MBean though, so let me demonstrate the Guice JMX support while configuring a Guice-managed object as an MBean. First, let's take a look at a simple MBean and its implementation, in Listings 7-18 and 7-19.

Listing 7-18. HelloMBean

```
package chapter7.jmx;

public interface HelloMBean {
    void sayHello();
}
```

Listing 7-19. HelloMBean Implementation

```
package chapter7.jmx;

import javax.management.JMException;
import javax.management.MBeanServer;
import javax.management.ObjectName;
import com.google.inject.Inject;

public class Hello implements HelloMBean {
    public void sayHello() {
        System.out.println("Hello JMX!");
    }

    @Inject
    public void registerThisBean(MBeanServer server) {
        try {
            server.registerMBean(
                this, new ObjectName("Guice Powered MBeans:type=Hello"));
        } catch (JMException e) {
            throw new RuntimeException(e);
        }
    }
}
```

Much like the collection registry code in the "Binding Collections" section, the MBean implementation in Listing 7-19 registers itself with the MBeanServer instance. Again, this has nothing to do with the Guice JMX integration; it is just code to register my own Guice-powered MBean.

When configuring the Injector, I bind MBeanServer so that HelloMBean can register itself. Next, I bind the HelloMBean as an eager singleton so that it registers itself at start-up. Listing 7-20 shows this code and the code that enables the Guice JMX support.

Listing 7-20. Guice with JMX

```
...
import com.google.inject.tools.jmx.Manager;
...
public class RunJMX {
    public static void main(String[] args) throws Exception {
        Injector injector = Guice.createInjector(new AbstractModule() {
            protected void configure() {
                // The MBeanServer you can use to register your own MBeans,
```

```
            // bound using toInstance for the sake of the example.
            // This is *not* needed for the Guice Manager.
            bind(MBeanServer.class)
                .toInstance(ManagementFactory.getPlatformMBeanServer());

            // Your own MBean
            bind(HelloMBean.class)
                .to(Hello.class)
                .asEagerSingleton();
        }
    });

    // Register Guice binding information as MBeans
    Manager.manage("Guice Binding Information", injector);

    // wait forever, so you can run jconsole
    Thread.sleep(Long.MAX_VALUE);
    }
}
```

The highlighted code in Listing 7-20 is all there is to say about the Guice JMX integration. That single command will register all the Injector's bindings as MBeans.

To test the JMX code, I put the application to sleep on the last line of the example, so that you have the time to open up the Java Monitoring and Management Console (jconsole), which is a JMX client that comes with Java SE. If you run that program while the code in Listing 7-20 is still running, you should be able to connect to it and see something like the results shown in Figure 7-2.

Figure 7-2. JMX in the Java Monitoring and Management Console

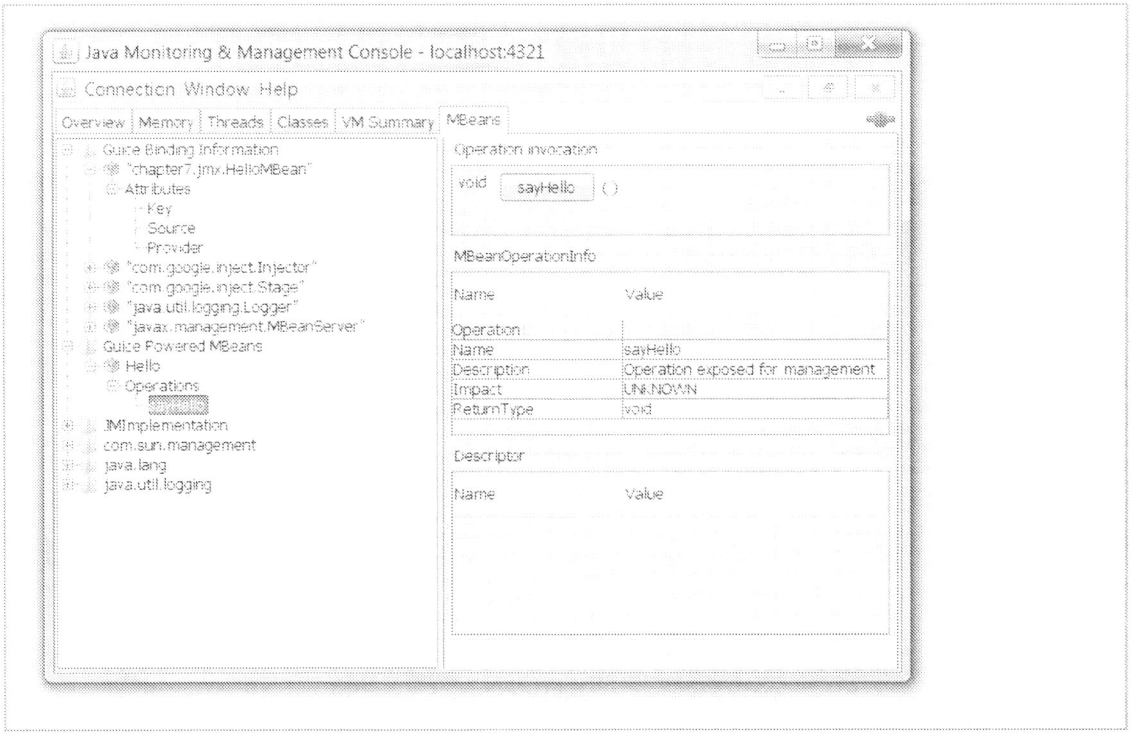

To quickly test this code in Eclipse, I ran the example code with the following JVM parameters, which allowed me to connect jconsole to the localhost:4321 location:

```
-Dcom.sun.management.jmxremote
-Dcom.sun.management.jmxremote.port=4321
-Dcom.sun.management.jmxremote.authenticate=false
-Dcom.sun.management.jmxremote.ssl=false
```

Summary

Some of your Guice knowledge can only come from experience with the framework. To give you a head start, this chapter presented you with several edge cases you might encounter when using Guice:

- Understanding Guice's singleton scope and how it differs from the classic singleton pattern

- Binding collections

- Designing libraries and limiting visibility

- Designing with large numbers of binding annotations

- Mixing scopes and scope widening

In addition to those topics, I also discussed various small extras that you can take advantage of when using Guice 1.0:

- Integrating with the Spring Framework

- Logging information that Guice produces

- Using JNDI with Guice

- Using JMX and inspecting bindings using JMX

This chapter concludes your Guice learning experience. As dessert, the next and final chapter will discuss what Guice's future currently looks like. If you're having a problem that I did not explain, maybe you'll see a solution in the next Guice release?

Chapter 8: The Future

Let's take a quick look at what the future has in store for Guice, in terms of feature sets as well general direction. This chapter presents information from a variety of sources like the Guice issue tracker and mailing list, online presentations, interviews, and Bob Lee himself.

None of this is set in stone, so don't come knocking on my door if I make any false predictions.

The Grand Plan

Now that Guice 1.0 has been out the door for a year or so and people have built great applications with it, the question is, "What should the Guice team do next?" Well, if you take a look at the Guice issue tracker on the project's web site, you'll see that there are plenty of ideas to choose from. But instead of going feature crazy, the Guice team tries to back each feature request with at least three use cases. As you can read on the project web site, when in doubt, they leave it out.

Most of the features currently under consideration can probably go in one the following six categories. Think of the first category as the overall theme.

- Growing an extensible platform
- Improving up-front checking
- Keeping Guice simple and making it simpler
- Improving tooling support
- Addressing DI shortcomings
- Maintaining top-notch performance

Let's talk about the first five categories in more detail and take a look at the planned improvements in those areas. There's nothing specific going on in the last category; I just put it in because Guice is designed with performance in mind. Who knows? Maybe we'll see Guice in a Java ME environment one day.

Note: Talking about ME, in the interview Bob Lee gave at Javapolis 2007 (`http://parleys.com`), he mentioned the possibility of generating (byte)code at compile time that would do what the `Injector` would normally do at runtime. In constrained environments like mobile platforms, this kind of precompilation is definitely an intriguing approach and takes the "up-front checking" mantra to the extreme.

Growing an Extensible Platform

Growing an extensible platform is the first and probably most important theme in the future of Guice. Instead of trying to be all things to all people, Guice aims to be first and foremost a platform that can be built on.

Bear with me for a moment, and try to see Guice as an abstraction over the DI concept. Then, I think there are two types of frameworks: the first type moves the level of abstraction up and the second type adds extra layers of abstraction. Let me illustrate with an example.

As soon as you're talking about a DI framework these days, people start asking for EJB support. That's valid, because, for example, as EJB has specified a simple DI mechanism since version 3.0. Comparable to Guice's `@Inject` annotation, EJB has an `@Resource` annotation that allows you to mark dependencies for injection. Now, if Guice was the first type of framework, it would just implement support for EJB's annotations and present that support to the outside world, no questions asked. This would be akin to driving the level of abstraction up.

But, as you can probably guess from this section's title, the Guice team prefers to add the *primitives* that allow users to solve this problem and all similar problems in one hit. These primitives or *added layers of abstraction* are what make Guice the second type of framework and thus a more extensible platform. In fact, it's likely that implementing something like EJB on top of Guice will become possible in the future, as I'll briefly explain next.

Note: I'm a huge fan of the design principle that says "simple things should be simple; complex things should be possible." And it seems to me that the Guice team is on the same page.

Among the interesting features that are on the table for addition to Guice are class and/or constructor listeners. It's not yet certain what form these will take, but you can compare these listeners to constructor interceptors, analogous to the method interceptors you saw in Chapter 4. You would, for example, register interceptors that get fired right before or after Guice creates a matching object (I'm guessing after). That would then allow you to do a whole range of things to the current object. For example, you could use reflection to get a list of fields and inject the ones that have the @Resource annotation on them. Seriously, this would be so powerful that Superman himself would wish he took classes in Java.

Note: Construction listeners would also enable application life cycle events like EJB's @PreDestroy or @PostConstruct functionality.

Better Up-Front Checking

With this second theme, I mean improvements to the extent that Guice can help you detect errors at start-up, or perhaps even at compile time, by moving as much risk as possible to the Java compiler. In case you're not sure what the latter means, Guice already helps you quite a bit with its Binding EDSL. For example, the compiler will not allow you to bind an interface to an incompatible class. There's a lot more thought behind this than you might think.

Looking at the previous section, you'll understand that the Guice team wants to make it easier for people to extend the core Guice platform. One area of improvement that they're currently looking at is configuration. For example, let's say you want to externalize Guice configuration in an XML file. This would involve generating a set of bindings and object interdependencies at runtime, probably using providers and Injector injection. Because these interdependencies would only get resolved at runtime, things might blow up rather late in the game. This is not ideal.

That's why the next version of Guice will allow you to get providers for a given type or key at configuration time (getProvider(...) methods inside modules). This will allow Guice to do better up-front checks, like discovering whether a dependency can be resolved when Guice starts. Instead of having your application blow up at runtime, Guice will tell you right away if you make an error.

As an interesting side effect, this will also allow you to pass in providers to any MethodInterceptor instances or Scope instances you create at configuration time. You'd still have to be careful though, especially in the case of interceptors, not to use a provider of a type that the interceptor itself intercepts, because that could lead to some nasty recursion. But hey, perhaps Guice could detect that, right?

Keeping Guice Simple and Making It Simpler

This category is where all the candy is. There are a number of exciting features on the table for the upcoming release, including these three likely candidates:

- Provider methods
- Finer grained optional dependencies, obtained by annotating an injection point with @Nullable
- Binding custom constant type converters

I'm particularly exited about the first feature, provider methods. Currently, to specify a provider, you need to create a subclass of the Provider instance and feed that to Guice. For simple cases, this introduces a lot of boilerplate code. I noticed this firsthand when I was building Guice integration for a third-party product; it depended a lot on factories for object creation, so I had to write a large number of providers.

The provider methods feature, on the other hand, doesn't require you to implement the Provider interface. Instead, it lets you specify provider code using regular Java methods on an arbitrary class or object. Let's take a look at an example in Listing 8-1; it might look familiar.

Listing 8-1. WebModule, Used in Chapter 6

```java
public class WebModule extends AbstractModule {
    @Override
    protected void configure() {
        bind(UserToken.class).toProvider(new Provider<UserToken>() {
            @Inject private HttpSession session;
            public UserToken get() {
                // Struts 2 synchronizes on the same object
                synchronized (session) {
                    return (UserToken) session.getAttribute(UserToken.KEY);
                }
            }
        }); // no scope!
    }
}
```

As you can see, having to write the Provider implementation introduces a considerable amount of boilerplate code. Using provider methods, you would implement this as shown in Listing 8-2.

Listing 8-2. WebModule Using Provider Methods

```java
public class WebModule extends AbstractModule {
    @Override
    protected void configure() {
        bindProviderMethods(this);
    }

    @Provides
    UserToken provideUserToken(HttpSession session) {
        return (UserToken) session.getAttribute(UserToken.KEY);
    }
}
```

Note that I made up the bindProviderMethods method, but what eventually makes it into Guice will look similar. Also specifying a class instead of an object will probably be possible.

In any case, Guice will look for methods annotated with @Provides on the class or object you specify and then generate the appropriate binding based on the return type of the method and, optionally, its scope annotation or binding annotation.

Applying scope annotations or binding annotations is as easy as you would expect. Listing 8-3 shows a more complete example.

Listing 8-3. Provide Grouchy Smurf with a White Cap

```
@Provides
@Singleton
@Grouchy
Smurf provideGrouchySmurf(@White Cap cap) {
    return new GrouchySmurf(cap);
}
```

Listing 8-3 would be equivalent to this Guice 1.0–style binding:

```
bind(Smurf.class)
    .annotatedWith(Grouchy.class)
    .toProvider(...)
    .in(Singleton.class);
```

Improved Tooling Support

Although you don't really need any tools to get productive with Guice, there are still some things that regular Java IDEs can't help you with. For example, you might want to inspect which bindings an Injector has configured and how the dependency graph looks. This is exactly what Guice's Service Provider Interface (SPI) will enable. In case you're not sure what an SPI is, it's like an API but for tools and larger platforms built on Guice. The SPI that will be in the next release is scheduled to contain the following two elements:

- An introspection SPI allowing you to inspect what Guice did at configuration time.

- A new Injector stage called Stage.TOOL that allows you to run Guice in a kind of superfast, simulation mode. This is ideal for tools that want to run Guice in the background and use the introspection SPI to determine what would happen if you ran Guice yourself.

Let me briefly introduce the introspection API. The central type in this SPI is BindingVisitor, which is an interface you need to implement to be able to inspect Guice's bindings after Injector creation. Listing 8-4 shows this interface in its current form.

Listing 8-4. *BindingVisitor in the Current Guice Trunk*

```
package com.google.inject.spi;

/**
 * Visits bindings. Pass an implementation of {@code BindingVisitor} to
 * {@link com.google.inject.Binding#accept(BindingVisitor)} and the binding
 * will call back to the appropriate visitor method for its type.
 *
 * @author crazybob@google.com (Bob Lee)
 */
public interface BindingVisitor<T> {
    void visit(LinkedBinding<? extends T> binding);
    void visit(InstanceBinding<? extends T> binding);
    void visit(ProviderInstanceBinding<? extends T> binding);
    void visit(LinkedProviderBinding<? extends T> binding);
    void visit(ProviderBinding<?> binding);
    void visit(ClassBinding<? extends T> binding);
    void visit(ConstantBinding<? extends T> binding);
    void visit(ConvertedConstantBinding<? extends T> binding);
}
```

To use this BindingVisitor, you pass it to the accept(...) method of a Binding. Listing 8-5 shows a small example of how you would visit all the explicit bindings in the current Injector.

Listing 8-5. *Using BindingVisitor*

```
Injector i = Guice.createInjector(new MyModule());
for (Binding<?> b : i.getBindings().values()) {
    b.accept(new DetectCircularDependenciesBindingVisitor());
}
```

A Guice IDE project is on its way that is directly related to the introspection SPI. As the name suggests, the project aims to deliver a Guice plug-in for popular IDEs like JetBrains's IntelliJ IDEA and Eclipse. It's still at a very early stage, but here are some of the key features:

- Finding bindings to a class

- Running an Injector in the background and detecting mistakes early

- Quick fix suggestions for Guice errors (planned)

- Guice refactorings (planned)

- Dependency graph visualization (planned)

To learn about this project's current progress, take a look at its web site at `http://code.google.com/p/guice-plugin/`.

Addressing DI Shortcomings

After reading this book, you'll definitely agree with me that DI is a godsend for Java and other languages in the C family. However, there are some shortcomings that most of the current approaches, including Guice's, don't address, two of which Guice will probably solve (and to some degree already solves):

- Mixing Guice-provided dependencies with dependencies provided at runtime
- The *robot legs* problem, that is, using two very similar object graphs with the same Injector

I already briefly mentioned the first problem in Chapter 3, "From Journeyman to Bob," in the "Providers" section. Currently, there are four solutions or workarounds, if you will, to this problem:

- Making your class mutable
- Using the Builder pattern
- Creating a factory
- Generating a factory using the AssistedInject Guice extension

Let's take a quick look at each one of these possible current solutions by means of an example. Take a look at Listing 8-6. Say you have a dog and want to take that dog for a walk.

Listing 8-6. Taking a Dog for a Walk

```java
public class Dog {}

public class Walk {
    private final Dog dog;
    private final boolean leash;

    @Inject
    public Walk(Dog dog, boolean leash) {
        this.dog = dog;
        this.leash = leash;
    }

    public void go() {}
}
```

Now, let's say that you want to decide whether you put the dog on a leash at the given moment when you start the walk, at runtime. That wouldn't work, because Guice creates the Dog object for you. You can't kinda create a Walk: either Guice creates a Walk or it doesn't.

The simplest solution would be to get the leash out of the constructor and add it as a setter, as shown in Listing 8-7.

Listing 8-7. Mutable Walk

```java
public class Walk {
    private final Dog dog;
    private boolean leash;

    @Inject
    public Walk(Dog dog) {
        this.dog = dog;
    }

    public void setLeash(boolean leash) {
        this.leash = leash;
    }

    public void go() {}
}
```

However, this is not ideal. Chances are that you're only going to set that value once and then no longer look at it. It's kind of a shame to make an object mutable, and deal with the possible threading issues and all, just because of this DI restriction you have.

The second option is to use the Builder pattern. By creating an *intermediate* object, you build up all the variables you need to construct a Walk and then create an immutable object in one go. This allows you to use Guice to set one part of the dependencies on the builder object and set the part that you don't know at runtime. Listing 8-8 shows an example Builder object, called WalkBuilder.

Listing 8-8. WalkBuilder

```java
public class WalkBuilder {
    private final Dog dog;
    private boolean leash;

    @Inject
    public WalkBuilder(Dog dog) {
        this.dog = dog;
    }

    public WalkBuilder setLeash(boolean leash) {
        this.leash = leash;
        return this;
    }

    public Walk build() {
        // return immutable instance
        return new Walk(dog, leash);
    }
}
```

Note: If you look closely, you'll notice that the Builder pattern is what Guice uses for its Binding EDSL.

Given an Injector i, you can use this WalkBuilder class to create an immutable Walk object as follows:

```java
Walk walk = i.getInstance(WalkBuilder.class).setLeash(true).build();
```

The third option is to use an intermediate factory class. Much like the builder approach, this requires you to create an intermediate object to put the Guice-provided dependencies in. Listing 8-9 shows this approach.

Listing 8-9. Intermediate Factory

```java
public interface WalkFactory {
    Walk create(boolean leash);
}

public class GuiceWalkFactory implements WalkFactory {
    private final Provider<Dog> dog;

    @Inject
    public GuiceWalkFactory(Provider<Dog> dog) {
        this.dog = dog;
    }

    public Walk create(boolean leash) {
        return new Walk(dog.get(), leash);
    }
}
```

Jesse Wilson and Jerome Mourits at Google elaborated on this last idea and created a Guice extension called AssistedInject. AssistedInject takes away some of the boilerplate code you have to write to solve this problem. All you have to do is annotate the assisted parameters on your constructor and then feed AssistedInject your factory interface. For example, take a look at Listing 8-10.

Listing 8-10. AssistedInject in Action

```java
public class Walk {
    private final Dog dog;
    private final boolean leash;

    @AssistedInject
    public Walk(Dog dog, @Assisted boolean leash) {
        this.dog = dog;
        this.leash = leash;
    }

    public void go() {}
}
```

```
public class AssistedMain {
    public static void main(String[] args) {
        Injector i = Guice.createInjector(new AbstractModule() {
            protected void configure() {
                bind(WalkFactory.class)
                    .toProvider(FactoryProvider.newFactory(
                                    WalkFactory.class, Walk.class));
            }
        });
        Walk walk = i.getInstance(WalkFactory.class).create(true);
    }
}
```

Although very useful, none of these solutions are ideal. A future version of Guice
will likely include a solution based on the ideas of the AssistedInject extension,
though what exactly that solution will be is uncertain yet. Perhaps there is even a
way to further automate this by, for example, generating code.

Note: If you want to take a look at AssistedInject, it's in the Guice trunk:
http://google-guice.googlecode.com/svn/trunk/extensions/assistedinject/. It's
probably best to take a look at the JavaDoc as well:
http://publicobject.com/publicobject/assistedinject/javadocs/index.html.

The second DI shortcoming, the robot legs problem, currently needs to be solved
by using two separate injectors. In the future, however, Guice will probably
support hierarchical injectors. This means that you will have child injectors,
much like you have child class loaders, each with a different variation of the
dependency graph. The Binding EDSL will then be extended to hide the details
of juggling multiple injectors, and you will be able to compose a dependency
graph by combining different injectors. The details are a bit sketchy at this point,
but they've got my vote.

Standardization

Guice, being purely Java based, shows what can really be done with DI in Java.
It's hard to imagine that you will still write factory-driven applications after
reading this book. Guice's influence is already showing up in Spring (version

2.5) and also in JSR 299, also known as Web Beans (http://jcp.org/en/jsr/detail?id=299). Web Beans is an interesting JSR that aims to provide glue between JSF and EJB and is heavily inspired by JBoss Seam and Guice. It's hard to say where this JSR will end up, but a lot of people have been pushing the Web Beans expert group to move the whole thing over to Java SE instead of just targeting Java EE. Other people oppose this, however. In any case, Gavin King (the expert group lead) has said that they aren't looking at including Web Beans in Java SE at this point, but it may well be a possibility later.

To take this Java SE inclusion idea even further, Bob Lee, who's also part of the Web Beans expert group, said he is currently working with some people on a JSR that will propose the addition of low-level DI plumbing to Java. As an analogy to class loaders (Java's ClassLoader), you could imagine having something like ObjectLoader that loads and injects objects. Such a system could then support higher level abstractions like Web Beans, Guice, and the Spring Framework. I can only imagine the possibilities: perhaps you could even annotate all of Java's libraries to support DI out of the box? Wouldn't it be nice if all the libraries in the Java space shipped fully annotated for use with your favorite DI framework?

I think the major theme here is that it's time to get DI into Java SE. Everyone keeps reinventing the same concept over and over again. EJB has a lightweight container; JSF has a lightweight container; then there's Spring, Seam, Web Beans, PicoContainer, Guice, and so on. It would be great if there were a lower level DI layer on which all these projects built, instead of constantly reinventing the wheel and making Java's learning curve ever steeper. Because, seriously, if you compare Java's learning curve to, for example, .NET's, it's just ridiculous what beginning programmers have to go through before they can get stuff done.

Note: Some people go even as far as calling @Inject the new *import*. I'm not one of those people, but it's still an interesting idea to think about. Check out Brian Slesinsky's blog post at http://slesinsky.org/brian/code/inject_is_the_new_import.html.

Summary

Guice is not only fun to use but aims to be an extensible platform. Most of the work going into the next release(s) can go into one of these categories:

- Growing an extensible platform
- Improving up-front checking
- Keeping Guice simple and making it simpler
- Improving tooling support
- Addressing DI shortcomings
- Maintaining top-notch performance

Looking further in the future, it will be interesting to see if Guice, or something like Guice, makes it into Java SE. I'm convinced it's time to take DI to the next level and unify all existing DI systems into a single extensible platform.

Appendix: Assorted Sweets

You're probably looking at this page right now because I referred you to it earlier in this book. While writing, I had to decide which examples fit in this book and which don't. This appendix captures the examples that I wanted to share with you even though they didn't fit into the flow of the book.

The first section briefly explains how you can roll your own API that captures Guice's Binding EDSL programming model.

The next three sections lay out source code that you can use to start building your own web applications using pure Guice, Wicket, or Warp Servlet. Again, I had to make a choice for the example chapter and went with Struts 2 in the end. If you're not a fan of Struts 2, these examples will satisfy your hunger.

Finally, the last section describes the interceptor you need to configure to use Warp Persist and Struts 2 with the session-per-request mode of operation. I use this interceptor in the Chapter 6 example, and I thought it would be a good idea to give you the details of the implementation.

Binder Syntax Explained

Although the style Guice uses for its configuration might look a bit magical, it's actually not that hard to reproduce. Consider this example:

```
binder.bind(FortuneService.class)
      .to(FortuneServiceImpl.class)
      .in(Scopes.SINGLETON);
```

Behind the scenes, the preceding code returns a builder object (of the GoF Builder pattern) between method calls that records the arguments given to the previous method calls. Using generics, the bind(...) method takes care of the type safety by passing the needed type information on to the builder object it returns. This ensures that the user will only be able to specify a compatible type in the to(...) method. Here's a simplified Binder implementation for the previous example:

```
public class Binder {
    private final List<BindingBuilder<?>> bindings =
        new ArrayList<BindingBuilder<?>>();

    public <T> BindingBuilder<T> bind(Class<T> clazz) {
        BindingBuilder<T> builder = new BindingBuilder<T>(clazz);
        bindings.add(builder);
        return builder;
    }

    // example usage
    public static void main(String[] args) {
        new Binder()
            .bind(FortuneService.class)
            .to(FortuneServiceImpl.class)
            .in(Scopes.SINGLETON);
    }
}
```

The BindingBuilder class is responsible for recording the to(...) and in(...) calls. At the end of the to(...) method, I return the current BindingBuilder object a second time (the first time is in Binder.bind(...)) so that I get the method chaining behavior I want.

```
public class BindingBuilder<T> {
    private Class<T> clazz;
    private Class<? extends T> impl;
    private Scope scope;

    public BindingBuilder(Class<T> clazz) {
        this.clazz = clazz;
    }

    public BindingBuilder<T> to(Class<? extends T> impl) {
        this.impl = impl;
        return this;
    }

    public void in(Scope scope) {
        this.scope = scope;
```

```
    }
    public Class<T> getClazz() {
        return clazz;
    }
    public Class<? extends T> getImpl() {
        return impl;
    }
    public Scope getScope() {
        return scope;
    }
}
```

Perhaps I could even throw an exception if the to(...) method gets called a
second time. But hey, it's just an example; feel free to expand it to fit your needs.

Hello Servlet Guice

As I explained in Chapter 5, it's not that hard to integrate Guice with the raw
servlets. This section gives to the source code to a simple "Hello, World!"
example that you can use to get your projects off the ground quickly:

- Listing A-1 sets up a Guice Module.

- Listing A-2 configures how Guice starts up.

- Listing A-3 creates an example servlet.

- Listing A-4 wires it all together in the web.xml file.

Listing A-1. HelloGuiceModule

```
package helloguice;
import com.google.inject.AbstractModule;
import com.google.inject.name.Names;

public class HelloGuiceModule extends AbstractModule {
    @Override
    protected void configure() {
        bindConstant().annotatedWith(Names.named("app.name"))
                    .to("Hello Servlet Guice");
    }
}
```

Listing A-2. GuiceServletContextListener

```java
package helloguice;

import javax.servlet.ServletContextEvent;
import javax.servlet.ServletContextListener;

import com.google.inject.Guice;
import com.google.inject.Injector;

public class GuiceServletContextListener implements ServletContextListener {
    public static final String KEY = Injector.class.getName();

    public void contextInitialized(ServletContextEvent sce) {
        sce.getServletContext().setAttribute(KEY, getInjector());
    }

    public void contextDestroyed(ServletContextEvent sce) {
        sce.getServletContext().removeAttribute(KEY);
    }

    private Injector getInjector() {
        return Guice.createInjector(new HelloGuiceModule());
    }
}
```

Listing A-3. HelloServlet

```java
package helloguice;
import java.io.IOException;
import java.io.PrintWriter;

import javax.servlet.ServletConfig;
import javax.servlet.ServletContext;
import javax.servlet.ServletException;
import javax.servlet.http.HttpServlet;
import javax.servlet.http.HttpServletRequest;
import javax.servlet.http.HttpServletResponse;

import com.google.inject.Inject;
import com.google.inject.Injector;
import com.google.inject.name.Named;
```

```java
public class HelloServlet extends HttpServlet {
    @Inject
    @Named("app.name")
    private String appName;

    @Override
    public void init(ServletConfig config) throws ServletException {
        super.init(config);
        ServletContext sc = config.getServletContext();
        Injector injector =
            (Injector) sc.getAttribute(GuiceServletContextListener.KEY);
        injector.injectMembers(this);
    }

    @Override
    public void doGet(HttpServletRequest req, HttpServletResponse resp)
                throws ServletException, IOException {
        resp.setContentType("text/html");
        PrintWriter writer = resp.getWriter();
        writer.printf("<h1>Welcome to the %s application!</h1>%n", appName);
        resp.setStatus(HttpServletResponse.SC_OK);
    }
}
```

Listing A-4. web.xml

```xml
<?xml version="1.0" encoding="UTF-8"?>
<web-app id="helloguice"
         version="2.4"
         xmlns="http://java.sun.com/xml/ns/j2ee"
         xmlns:xsi="http://www.w3.org/2001/XMLSchema-instance"
         xsi:schemaLocation="http://java.sun.com/xml/ns/j2ee
                             http://java.sun.com/xml/ns/j2ee/web-app_2_4.xsd">
    <display-name>Hello Guice</display-name>
    <listener>
        <listener-class>
            helloguice.GuiceServletContextListener
        </listener-class>
    </listener>
```

```
    <servlet>
        <servlet-name>welcome</servlet-name>
        <servlet-class>helloguice.HelloServlet</servlet-class>
    </servlet>
    <servlet-mapping>
        <servlet-name>welcome</servlet-name>
        <url-pattern>/*</url-pattern>
    </servlet-mapping>
</web-app>
```

Hello Wicket Guice

Much like the previous "Hello Servlet Guice" example, this example shows you
how to build a simple "Hello, World!" application but this time using the Apache
Wicket (http://wicket.apache.org) framework. You can reuse this example,
shown in Listings A-5 to A-9, to start building your own Guice-enabled Wicket
application.

Listing A-5. HelloGuiceApplication

```
package hellowicket;

import helloguice.HelloGuiceModule;

import org.apache.wicket.guice.GuiceComponentInjector;
import org.apache.wicket.protocol.http.WebApplication;

public class HelloGuiceApplication extends WebApplication {
    @Override
    public Class<?> getHomePage() {
        return Welcome.class;
    }
}
```

Listing A-6. A Welcome Page

```
package hellowicket;

import org.apache.wicket.markup.html.WebPage;
import org.apache.wicket.markup.html.basic.Label;

import com.google.inject.Inject;
import com.google.inject.name.Named;
```

```java
public class Welcome extends WebPage {
    @Inject @Named("app.name") private String appName;

    public Welcome() {
        add(new Label("welcome",
                        String.format("Welcome to the %s application!", appName)));
    }
}
```

Listing A-7. WicketModule

```java
package hellowicket;

import helloguice.HelloGuiceModule;
import org.apache.wicket.protocol.http.WebApplication;
import com.google.inject.AbstractModule;

public class WicketModule extends AbstractModule {
    @Override
    protected void configure() {
        bind(WebApplication.class).to(HelloGuiceApplication.class);
        install(new HelloGuiceModule());
    }
}
```

Listing A-8. HellogGuiceModule

```java
package helloguice;
import com.google.inject.AbstractModule;
import com.google.inject.name.Names;

public class HelloGuiceModule extends AbstractModule {
    @Override
    protected void configure() {
        bindConstant().annotatedWith(Names.named("app.name"))
                        .to("Hello Wicket Guice");
    }
}
```

Listing A-9. web.xml

```xml
<?xml version="1.0" encoding="UTF-8"?>
<web-app id="hellowicket"
        version="2.4"
        xmlns="http://java.sun.com/xml/ns/j2ee"
        xmlns:xsi="http://www.w3.org/2001/XMLSchema-instance"
        xsi:schemaLocation="http://java.sun.com/xml/ns/j2ee
                        http://java.sun.com/xml/ns/j2ee/web-app_2_4.xsd">
```

```
        <display-name>Wicket Guice</display-name>
        <filter>
            <filter-name>WicketFilter</filter-name>
            <filter-class>
                org.apache.wicket.protocol.http.WicketFilter
            </filter-class>
            <init-param>
                <param-name>applicationFactoryClassName</param-name>
                <param-value>
                    org.apache.wicket.guice.GuiceWebApplicationFactory
                </param-value>
            </init-param>
            <init-param>
                <param-name>module</param-name>
                <param-value>
                    hellowicket.WicketModule
                </param-value>
            </init-param>
            <init-param>
                <param-name>configuration</param-name>
                <!-- deployment or development -->
                <param-value>deployment</param-value>
            </init-param>
        </filter>
        <filter-mapping>
            <filter-name>WicketFilter</filter-name>
            <url-pattern>/*</url-pattern>
        </filter-mapping>
    </web-app>
```

Hello Warp Servlet

This section presents you with a code example that uses the advanced counterpart of Guice's raw servlet support. Warp Servlet, cousin to Warp Persist and the other projects over at http://www.wideplay.com, allows you to inject into servlets and filters as if they were regular classes. Listings A-10 to A-13 show you how you can use Warp Servlet to configure and inject a simple "Hello, World!" servlet.

Listing A-10. web.xml

```xml
<?xml version="1.0" encoding="UTF-8"?>
<web-app id="hellowarp"
        version="2.4"
        xmlns="http://java.sun.com/xml/ns/j2ee"
        xmlns:xsi="http://www.w3.org/2001/XMLSchema-instance"
        xsi:schemaLocation="http://java.sun.com/xml/ns/j2ee
                            http://java.sun.com/xml/ns/j2ee/web-app_2_4.xsd">

    <display-name>Hello Warp Servlet</display-name>
    <filter>
        <filter-name>WebFilter</filter-name>
        <filter-class>com.wideplay.warp.servlet.WebFilter</filter-class>
    </filter>
    <filter-mapping>
        <filter-name>WebFilter</filter-name>
        <url-pattern>/*</url-pattern>
    </filter-mapping>
    <listener>
        <listener-class>
            warpservlet.HelloGuiceServletContextListener
        </listener-class>
    </listener>
</web-app>
```

Listing A-11. HelloGuiceModule

```java
package helloguice;

import com.google.inject.AbstractModule;
import com.google.inject.name.Names;

public class HelloGuiceModule extends AbstractModule {
    @Override
    protected void configure() {
        bindConstant().annotatedWith(Names.named("app.name"))
                    .to("Hello Warp Servlet");
    }
}
```

Listing A-12. HelloGuiceServletContextListener

```
package warpservlet;

import helloguice.HelloGuiceModule;

import com.google.inject.Guice;
import com.google.inject.Injector;
import com.wideplay.warp.servlet.Servlets;
import com.wideplay.warp.servlet.WarpServletContextListener;

public class HelloGuiceServletContextListener extends WarpServletContextListener {
    @Override
    protected Injector getInjector() {
        return Guice.createInjector(
                new HelloGuiceModule(),
                Servlets.configure()
                        .filters()
                        .servlets().serve("/*").with(HelloServlet.class)
                        .buildModule());
    }
}
```

Listing A-13. HelloServlet

```
package warpservlet;

import java.io.IOException;
import java.io.PrintWriter;

import javax.servlet.ServletException;
import javax.servlet.http.HttpServlet;
import javax.servlet.http.HttpServletRequest;
import javax.servlet.http.HttpServletResponse;

import com.google.inject.Inject;
import com.google.inject.name.Named;
```

```java
public class HelloServlet extends HttpServlet {
    private final String appName;
    @Inject
    public HelloServlet(@Named("app.name") String appName) {
        this.appName = appName;
    }

    @Override
    public void doGet(HttpServletRequest req, HttpServletResponse resp)
                    throws ServletException, IOException {
        resp.setContentType("text/html");
        PrintWriter writer = resp.getWriter();
        writer.printf("<h1>Welcome to the %s application!</h1>%n", appName);
        resp.setStatus(HttpServletResponse.SC_OK);
    }
}
```

SessionPerRequestInterceptor

As discussed in Chapter 6, "Practical Guice," Warp Persist's
SessionPerRequestFilter class doesn't work with Struts 2 and the current Guice
plug-in. To overcome that problem, you need to use the
SessionPerRequestInterceptor class in Listing A-14. Note that the package
location matters, because the interceptor uses package private resources from
Warp Persist.

Listing A-14. SessionPerRequestInterceptor

```java
package com.wideplay.warp.jpa;

import javax.persistence.EntityManagerFactory;

import com.google.inject.Inject;
import com.google.inject.Provider;
import com.opensymphony.xwork2.ActionInvocation;
import com.opensymphony.xwork2.interceptor.Interceptor;
import com.wideplay.warp.persist.PersistenceService;

/**
 * For use with Warp-Persist. Needed because Guice's current
 * Struts 2 plugin creates the Guice Injector internally, thus is
 * not available to other filters before the Struts filter executes.
 * http://groups.google.com/group/warp-core/browse_thread/thread/738a8ce3c7275602/.
 * <p>
 * After serialization this class will currently fail to close down the JPA
```

```java
 * {@link EntityManagerFactory} properly.
 *
 * @author Robbie Vanbrabant
 */
public class SessionPerRequestInterceptor implements Interceptor {
    private static final long serialVersionUID = -3463189373921935923L;
    // not Serializable
    private transient Provider<EntityManagerFactory> emfProvider;

    @Inject
    public SessionPerRequestInterceptor(Provider<EntityManagerFactory> emfp) {
        // only use after the PersistenceService starts
        this.emfProvider = emfp;
    }

    public String intercept(ActionInvocation ai) throws Exception {
        EntityManagerFactoryHolder.getCurrentEntityManager();
        try {
            return ai.invoke();
        } finally {
            EntityManagerFactoryHolder.closeCurrentEntityManager();
        }
    }

    /**
     * @see com.opensymphony.xwork2.interceptor.Interceptor#init()
     */
    public void init() {}

    /**
     * @see com.opensymphony.xwork2.interceptor.Interceptor#destroy()
     */
    public void destroy() {
        if (emfProvider != null) {
            EntityManagerFactory emf = emfProvider.get();
            synchronized(emf) {
                if (emf.isOpen()) emf.close();
            }
        }
    }
}
```

```
// This could use optional=true by requiring a binding annotation;
// then users could choose whether the interceptor starts the
// PersistenceService or not.
@Inject
public void start(PersistenceService service) {
    // this is a good place to start the persistence service
    // for this to work, but you need to make sure that you only
    // have 1 (one) interceptor-ref to this interceptor. You can do this
    // by creating an interceptor-stack with this interceptor, and then
    // reference it through that single-interceptor stack.
    // Struts 2 creates one interceptor instance per interceptor-ref,
    // and the Guice plugin currently does not support scoping them.
    service.start();
}
}
```

Caution: When you use SessionPerRequestInterceptor you must *not* include Warp Persist's SessionPerRequestFilter in the web.xml file.

As you can read in the comments for the start(...) method in Listing A-14, you need to make sure only one instance of the Interceptor exists. Struts 2 interceptors *appear* to be singletons (as in single instance per application), but in reality, there is one instance per <interceptor-ref> tag in your configuration. To work around that, you can create an interceptor stack with only SessionPerRequestInterceptor in it and reference that stack from then on. First, you'll need to configure something like Listing A-15.

Listing A-15. A Single-Interceptor Interceptor Stack

```
<interceptors>
    <interceptor name="sessionPerRequestInterceptor"
        class="com.wideplay.warp.jpa.SessionPerRequestInterceptor"/>
    <!-- Stack with single interceptor because we only want one instance -->
    <!-- Interceptors = one instance per interceptor-ref -->
    <interceptor-stack name="spriStack">
        <interceptor-ref name="sessionPerRequestInterceptor" />
    </interceptor-stack>
</interceptors>
```

Note: Why not use Guice to scope the `Interceptor`? As I mentioned in Chapter 5, the Struts 2 Guice plug-in is currently not able to scope **Struts** interceptors. By now, you probably understand why.

Once you've created your custom stack, you can simply use it as shown in Listing A-16. This is the actual code from the Shopping List example application discussed in Chapter 6.

Listing A-16. Using the spriStack

```
<interceptor-stack name="securedStack">
    <interceptor-ref name="spriStack" />
    <interceptor-ref name="authenticationInterceptor" />
    <interceptor-ref name="defaultStack" />
</interceptor-stack>
```

Copyright

Printed in the United States
111145LV00003B